Crafting Pagan Rituals

Blacksun

ISBN – 13:   978-1492360810
ISBN – 10:   1492360813

For all who
dispense the sacraments of
Life, Light, and Love.

My deepest appreciation to the countless
number of teachers, friends, mentors, and
students who have increased my
understanding along the way.

Beauty is Spirit

PROLOGUE
[THE SPELL OF MAKING]

The following is from my book, *The Spell of Making*, published in 1995. That work was also about the art of crafting Pagan rituals. Over the years, I've thought about rewriting that book, trying to make it read better, be more compact. But other projects always seemed to get in the way. Now, I've decided to present the information in a somewhat different fashion than I did in that work. My ability to express myself in print has improved over the years and my understanding of the subject material has also been helped by the countless times I've presented it in classes and seminars.

This story was the prologue to that book and inspired its title. It is only partially fictional. As they say in movie trailers, it is based on true incidents. Everything portrayed in this story has actually occurred with one exception [it wasn't a cave]. I have helped present this ritual/spell many times and hope to do so for many years more. It is, to my way of thinking, one of my best rituals. This is The Spell of Making:

The acolytes emerge from the fourth phase of their initiation into a large chamber of the cave. Dark and mysterious at the outer edges, the tiny candles on the four altars in the center are beacons of hope and reality to the tearful and anxious group that gathers just inside the chamber's entry.

It has been a long and tiring journey for them all. Their choices since that morning have finally led them to this vast underground room with a simple candle-lit circle in the middle of the darkness. Their guides, who have led them through the perils and frightening revelations of the past hours now whisper words of encouragement in their ears and leave them, slipping into the shadows along the perimeter of the cavern.

i

An old woman stands in the circle, slowly going from one altar to the next, muttering, chuckling, and fussing with articles on each. She seems unaware of the growing group of young hopefuls who gather a few yards away, watching her every move and wondering what their part will be in this next piece of magic. Their bodies and senses are nearly numb from the hours of tension and work they have had to go through. What else would they have to endure?

The last acolyte is brought into the large hall. His guide whispers for him to stand ready and then disappears into the shadows like the rest of the guides before him. The small murmurings from the shadows fall into silence as the old woman turns and faces the frightened group. For a long moment she looks at them with unblinking eyes. In their sight, she seems to grow straighter and taller as she studies them. She picks up a gnarled wand, dark with age, highly polished from handling, and with a silver tip. Then she speaks.

"This is the final step in your transformation. Since the sun set and the full moon shone on the Eastern horizon this evening, you have wandered in these caves and faced the most frightening aspects of the universe. Those who have not turned back or *been* turned back are here now. To you all, I give greetings.

"What you are about to learn here is the greatest spell you shall ever be taught. It is the very key to all magic and its knowledge is a dangerous thing in the wrong hands. If you feel comfortable learning it, please sit down on the floor of the cave now."

For 19 heartbeats the old woman looks with a sharp eye at the group of acolytes. On the twentieth, a young girl sits down and looks at the others standing around her. A small smile begins to form on her lips. Then she looks back to the light in the middle of the cave. Tears come into the eyes of the old woman as she looks back at the girl. If only she had waited for the required 21 pulses! With a catch in her voice, the woman says to her, **"You may leave."**

The young girl looks around in confusion as her guide materializes from the shadows and helps her to stand and be led away. All eyes follow the girl as she begins to quietly weep for her loss. The rest watch her go, wondering what she had done wrong.

"To learn...," says the old woman, **"especially to learn something which you have just been told is a great and dangerous**

spell... will forever change you. To change is to experience pain. Those who are at ease with feeling their own pain will feel comfortable giving pain. They must not know such secrets." She lets her message sink in for a moment. Then she wipes her eyes dry and says with a deep sigh, "Let us continue."

Picking up a broom, the old woman begins sweeping the floor within the boundary of the altars.

"Red spirits and black, white spirits and gray: come ye, come ye, come who may." The words are echoed from the shadows as she says them. A faint stirring of the air is felt by all and the candle flames begin to lean first one way then the other in time with the words. There seems to be many more voices from the shadows surrounding the circle than could be accounted for by just the guides that disappeared into the darkness moments before. The acolytes, five in all now, unconsciously huddle together.

"Around and about, through in and throughout, the good come in and the ill *KEEP OUT!*"

There is a thunderous stamping of the feet from everywhere in the cavern on the last two words and the echo of this is heard returning from the caves that are part of the system they have wandered all night: "*KEEP OUT... KEEP OUT... KEEP OUT....*"

The young people frantically look into the darkness that surrounds them and gather even closer for comfort. When they turn their attention back to the circle, three others have joined in the light with the old woman: two men and a young woman, hardly older than the oldest of the group that awaits their fate. The older man carries a sword whose blade catches the candle light and seems to amplify it around the cave. As it flashes, the acolytes glimpse many robed figures around the entire perimeter of the cave. He lifts the sword above the altar in the East, inscribes a sigil and begins to slowly draw a circle with the blade tip pointing straight out. His words ring clear and strong in the now hushed arena.

"Oh thou circle, be thou a meeting place of Love and Trust, a shield against all evil which shall protect and contain the energies we raise within thee." He has returned the sword to over the East altar, but now raises it to point straight up in the center of the circle. "All this we ask in the names of the Lord and the Lady... MOTE IT BE!"

"**MOTE IT BE!**" say the people from the darkness. Once again, the echoes of their answering words resound from the cave walls and the acolytes look about them, wondering just how many more people are really in the cave with them. The man with the sword has driven it down into the dirt in the exact center of the circle. Now he lifts it back up, wipes the blade tip on his sleeve, and hands it to the younger man. It is placed under an altar in a scabbard. Then the young man pulls a double edged blade from his robes and goes to the East altar. He makes a sign with the blade over the altar and says something that the acolytes can't quite hear. This is repeated over each of the altars and finally the man turns to the old woman, says something quietly to her, and then goes to stand in front of the Southern altar.

Next, the young woman steps into the center of the circle. The candle light is reflected in her sparkling eyes and falls softly on her fair face and form. She is the very picture of youth and beauty and her smile is pleasure itself. Her words ring sweet and clear.

"**The work of this night will be done within a sacred circle of Love and Trust. All who are here must be so of their own true will in harmony with the gods and one another. If anyone has reservations about another, let them say so now, so we may make peace.**" She waits and slowly turns around the circle, looking and listening. The young man comes to her side and looks into the darkness. "**Is there Peace on the circle?**" he asks in a clear, strong voice. He turns 90 degrees and asks the same question. Again, and yet again, he asks as he turns facing each direction. None say that they are not at peace.

"**My lady,**" the young woman says to the crone, "**we are at peace.**" She returns to stand in front of the altar in the West and the young man returns to the South. The old woman gestures to her older male counterpart and he draws his own double edged blade and describes a portal at the Northeast section of the circle, directly in front of the group of acolytes. The old woman goes to this portal, holds out her hand toward the group and says, "**Come.**"

Slowly, haltingly, the five approach the lighted circle. But just as the first of them is about to enter into the area, the old woman holds up her hand to stop them. She looks at the first and gives the traditional challenge: "**What do you bring to this circle?**"

"**I bring Perfect Love and Perfect Trust,**" replies the acolyte. He is allowed to pass into the circle and the next is challenged in the same manner. As each enters, they are given a length of thin, strong cording equal to the distance from one shoulder to another of that person and told to stand in front of the East altar. Finally, all have been admitted and the portal is sealed once again by the older man, who then goes to stand at the Northern altar.

The old woman stands in the center of the circle and speaks to the acolytes. "**Each of the four altars on this circle represents one of the four elements of old: Air in the East, Fire in the South, Water in the West, and Earth in the North. Though other traditions may change the positions of these elements, their meaning and purpose remain the same. They are the keys to all magic, all truth, all power in your lives.**

"**You create your reality... each of you, every moment. That which is in your universe is in you and comes through you. To know this is to be responsible *to* this universe and to be honest to yourself and to your gods. The *Spell of Making* is the spell that is at the heart of all other spell work. It is the alpha and omega of your magic, your universe, and your true self. To make your universe and everything in it, you must work this spell, so you have already done so countless times in this life and others. Now it shall be made clear to you and you shall have a reminder of its power.**"

The old woman points to the four altars and continues. "**Each of the altars contains a different colored bead for you to take and put onto your cords. When you are done, you will have a simple reminder of the power and responsibility each of you has at your fingertips. Turn and face the altar in back of you. As in all spells, we begin in the East.**"

The group turns and looks at a simple platform that contains various articles and tools usually associated with the element of Air. From the darkness come the whispers of many voices:

"**This is The Spell of Making:**"

The old woman speaks from behind them:

"**This is the East, the altar of the Air Element, symbol of your intelligence and inspiration. May the winds blow away the cloudiness from your mind. All things begin with your thoughts. Worship at this altar often, for what you think is what you become.**

"Take a token from this altar and put it on your cord so you may be reminded of the power of this element. Then go to the South altar. This is The Spell of Making."

When the five have taken their bead and moved to the next altar, once again come the whispers:

"This is The Spell of Making:"

It is the young man that stands beside that altar who speaks:

"This is the South, the altar of the Fire Element, symbol of energy. Control your energy, lest it burn you. You must put energy to your thoughts, for no matter how brilliant, without energy they would be but wisps of wind. Worship at this altar often, for without energy, there can be neither life nor change.

"Take a token from this altar and put it on your cord so you may be reminded of the power of this element. Then go to the West altar. This is The Spell of Making."

They gather around the West altar and once again the whispers, as one voice, come from the dark:

"This is The Spell of Making:"

Now it is the young woman's turn to speak, saying:

"This is the West, the altar of the Water Element, symbol of our emotions. May your waters run free and be sparkling and pure. All ideas which have been given energy must pass through this element or they have no meaning. Worship at this altar often, for a life without emotion is as dry as dust.

"Take a token from this altar and put it on your cord so you may be reminded of the power of this element. Then go to the North altar. This is The Spell of Making."

Once again, as they assemble at the next altar and the whispers come from out of the darkness:

"This is The Spell of Making:"

The old man speaks to them:

"This is the North, the altar of the Earth Element, symbol of fertility, measurement, and what is called reality. All things which have been thought, given energy, and made meaningful by your emotions are of value to neither yourself nor anyone else if not made real. But remember: what you make real, you are responsible for.

Worship at this altar often, for a life is incomplete and without value if not real.

"Take a token from this altar and put it on your cord so you may be reminded of the power of this element. Then go to the center of the circle. This is The Spell of Making."

They take their tokens and thread them onto the cords. As they gather in the center, the cave echoes as if with a thousand voices saying:

"This is The Spell of Making:"

The old woman approaches them once again and says:

"The BALANCE between your Air, your Fire, your Water, and your Earth is the key to the Fifth Element: the Element of Spirit. Keep the Balance and your Spirit will grow. The altar of the Spirit Element is in the center of the circle.

You are the center of the circle; *you* are the Altar of the Spirit.

To grow in spirituality, keep the Wheel turning and keep it balanced."

"This is The Spell of Making:"

"Guard this knowledge and keep it sacred, for it is the greatest spell you shall learn. This *is* The Spell of Making."

[1]
Building Rituals

This is a book about creating ritual, what is sometimes called *ritual craft*. You will find a few rituals within its covers, but they will be only for illustrative purposes. You certainly may use parts of these sample rituals for your own purposes if that is your desire but the whole reason for this book is to teach you how to make rituals that completely reflect *your own ideas*. Each person has a unique vision of what is sacred and the spiritual rituals you create should reflect that vision.

We all do rituals for many different aspects of our lives. In fact, it's quite possible that there isn't anything that humans do that does not have rituals incorporated with the activity. This book will focus on spiritual rituals even though the principles and information you will be given are just as true for social, personal, or any other kind of ritual. I will use examples from rituals that I have crafted to demonstrate the principles and techniques you will learn here. I am a priest of Wicca, so the rituals will be Wiccan and the explanations and lessons will use the vernacular of my eclectic Pagan perspectives. But these principles and techniques are universal to all religions. The only difference being which symbols are used and the vocabulary or vernacular of the faith group.

It doesn't matter what religion the ritual is designed for. The process of constructing it will follow the same principles. That being said, however, it should also be noted that any particular spirituality, the "brand of religion" that requires the ritual, will have a tremendous effect on the look and tone of the ritual. The personal symbology and beliefs of the people who attend the ritual also will have a great impact on the way the ritual is performed and how its meaning will be interpreted.

Every part of a ritual will produce a wide range of variables which will determine the outcome. Also, it can't ever be performed exactly the same way twice, so you will never have *total* control over the results. But you will be able to construct rituals that have an excellent chance of changing the lives of the people who attend them. It is a big responsibility and this work will help you create solid, powerful, and meaningful rituals.

Constructing a ritual is not a precise, strait forward piece of work. It isn't something that follows a highly organized plan like a blueprint is for building a house. Ritual construction is an art. It's unpredictable in many ways and creating one is a mentally and emotionally taxing job. If you have been called upon to create a spiritually important rite for others, you would be a fool if you didn't feel the weight of responsibility. But take heart, this book will give you a solid foundation to work from and a knowledge of what makes up a complete and powerful ritual.

Will all of your rituals be masterpieces? Will they all go on to be honored by notables within your faith group? Not likely. I have been writing rituals for nearly forty years and can count on one hand the ones that came above the "Fine" mark. However, because I know the principles and methods that you will learn in this book, the number of rituals I've constructed that fall below the "Good" mark are even less.

Because ritual construction is an art, it is highly subjective and there is absolutely nothing that can replace practice. What you create at first you will probably consider naïve or inadequate when you have had more opportunities to create rituals in the future. But you will have had to make those baby steps before you could walk or run with your art. And, believe it or not, after you've practiced this art long enough, you will look upon those early works with more loving eyes, knowing how they reflect a simple and pure spirit that is almost always more difficult to find in more sophisticated works.

As mentioned at the beginning of this chapter, this will not be a book full of rituals that you can copy into your own journal and use. It isn't a book full of *pieces* of rituals that you can slide and twist into a picture puzzle rite. If you don't wish to learn the art of ritual construction, don't bother reading further; the rest of this book will not be of use to you. I liken the situation to the difference between a cookbook and learning how to cook.   This is not a cookbook.

Let's start cooking.

[2]
Looking for Meaning

If we were learning about making automobiles, the first thing you would have to know is how an automobile worked. What made it go, what made it stop, and what made it do all the other things you wanted it to do. Without such knowledge it would be ridiculous to expect you to build a car that worked, let alone one that worked well. To stretch this analogy a little more, just think how long it took for humans to invent the wheel.

Fortunately, you do have a couple of pieces of information about ritual that can help you understand how it works. You know that rituals...

1. Are used for a wide variety of human activities.
2. Are more than just fancy gatherings.
3. And are sometimes not very rational activities.

The two biggest categories of ritual are *social* and *spiritual*. A simple example of a social ritual is a birthday party. And, of course, spiritual rituals abound and we all can relate to a dedication or an initiation to a particular variety of religion. How are these two examples alike and how do they differ?

Both rituals focus on an event or action on an individual. Even if the initiation rite is done for several people at the same time, it is designed to affect each person separately. Birthday celebrations focus on the meaning for each individual even if the celebration is for more than one person. So we can see that these rituals are performed to affect individuals. This doesn't mean that the ritual can't be performed for many individuals at the same time and in the same place, only that they are designed to make a difference to individuals.

Another similarity would be symbology. Both rituals use many symbols that convey a complex message to the individual. The spiritual ritual might send a message of belonging, a change in status or identity that proclaims a specific form of union with the divine as defined by the tenets of that religion. The birthday ritual

4

also uses symbology [cake, presents, songs, etc.] designed to convince the birthday boy or girl that they are special and have crossed over into a higher status [one year older]. Both rituals have similar meanings but in very different contexts. Also, both rituals use multiple cultural symbols, some of which are reserved specifically for that ritual.

One glaring difference between the two rituals is the fact that the birthday ritual is commonly performed on a person many times in their life but the confirmation or initiation rite is often meant to be performed only once. In some traditions, initiations are tailored to the specific individual and can be vastly different between one initiate and the next. Birthday parties can also be seen as being personally tailored, but normally aren't very different from one to the next within the same culture.

Before we get into how to make a ritual, we need to look at how rituals work. What makes them go and stop and do the hoodoo that they do? To discover all that, we need to look at three things:

1. Thinking. What is this thing we call thinking? Are our thoughts all the same type of activity?
2. Symbology. What are symbols, what function do they play in our thinking, and how are they employed in rituals?
3. Reality. What is real? How do we decide? Do emotions affect reality?

But before any of that, there's one question that needs to be addressed:

Just what the heck *is* a ritual, anyway?

[3]
Definitions

What is a ritual? In my youth [before they invented rocks], I spent almost a whole year trying to get an answer to that question. I went around to a bunch of churches and temples and even to a college campus asking various wise men and women what a ritual was. The answers were almost contradictory in some cases and many were completely out in left field. In one instance, I was told in no uncertain terms that I should not pursue such knowledge beyond a dictionary meaning and most certainly should avoid [oh, heaven forbid!] *doing* any rituals whatsoever! Then the same guy invited me come to his church that Sunday and partake of Communion and, by the way, had I been baptized? I know: some things are just too funny for words.

Rather than give a bunch of long, drawn-out arguments about some of the definitions I've heard and read over the years, let me give you an easy explanation of what a ritual is and what it is supposed to do. I think this will cover about 99% of the instances where the word is used [accurately] and keep the static down over a lot of extraneous chatter about the subject.

A ritual is an activity of the mind symbolically manifested in the physical world by a person or persons.

Rituals are used to carry information to the unconscious mind without having to be translated from a rational form to the form used by the unconscious mind.

These two sentences are critical to understanding how to create an effective ritual. They also will help when presenting one.

One of the biggest inaccuracies concerning rituals is that they need to be repeated. There is also a kind of backwards version of this same misunderstanding whereby almost anything that is repeated over and over is dubbed a ritual. The number of repetitions something is done has nothing to do with it being a ritual. And, to be 100% accurate, rituals are done only once because, as you will see, it is impossible to do a ritual in the *exact* same way twice. Simply changing the time, the place, the people, or any of the millions of other factors involved in performing the ritual changes it. So it might accurately be stated that all rituals are done only once.

Of course, though that is technically true, it doesn't negate the fact that rituals are *often* presented more than once. It also doesn't mean that really good spiritual rituals should not be carefully planned and presented. There are some within the modern Pagan faith groups who claim that the best rituals are spontaneous affairs, often arising from a collection of people who quite probably have little knowledge of the difference between a ritual and a celebratory small and localized riot.

Obviously, I do not subscribe to such a view. While the general tone of many Pagan gatherings is a happy and free attitude, to believe that it is the source of all our spiritual truths and the sole generator of our sacraments would reduce our faith group to nothing more than a hodge-podge of delirious and irrelevant revelers. As an ex-hippy who spent a good number of mornings wondering what happened the night before, let me assure you that it isn't as great as it first sounds.

Producing rituals that support our spiritual journeys and promote a harmonious and fuller association between our individual spirits and the gods [*no matter how we view them*] is the duty and privilege of the priesthood of our spiritualties. From one tradition to the next, exactly who makes up that priesthood differs wildly. But the general job description usually centers around the notion that the priest or priestess is a seeker of spiritual understanding. It is their job to become better at knowing themselves and their relationship with the gods. Because we are not a cloistered group, our journey usually includes dispensing the sacraments to and with other like-minded seekers. And that ultimately means we will be doing rituals with them.

Even if we were separated from the rest of humanity, our lives would still contain many, many rituals. And, as long as we maintained even the smallest interest in matters of the spirit, some of those rituals would be spiritual rites.

So, as stated earlier, rituals are mental activities *symbolically* portrayed in the physical world for the purpose of transmitting information directly to the unconscious in a form that does not require the usual "translation" that constitutes the normal feedback process from the conscious mind. That needs a little translation of its own:

For the moment, let's ignore the so called *sub*-conscious. The conscious and unconscious minds handle information in completely different ways. Consider this: How many airplanes have passed overhead in the last hour? Even in the dead of night, it would be quite a few unless you were in an extremely remote part of the world. Of course, you probably can't answer the question because you weren't paying *conscious* attention. However, the faint sounds of those airplanes could be heard if you were paying attention. What is the difference? You might answer, "I *did* pay conscious attention and I became *aware* of the sounds." Yes, that is correct. But what really happened to change things? Certainly the sounds didn't change. And neither did your ears.

What changed was your attention. The sound entered your ears whether you were consciously aware of it or not. And it could be proven that the sound was converted by the structures of the ear into nerve impulses that went to the same area of the brain whether you were conscious of them or not. In fact, what happened to those sounds for the first couple of microseconds had nothing to do with whether you were conscious of them or not. If you weren't consciously aware of the sounds, you nevertheless heard them. If we were to put a tiny probe into the right part of the brain and give it a very tiny squirt of electricity, you would "hear" the sounds. They were stored in the brain but you were never aware of them. Consciously.

What happened to those sounds is typical of nearly all of the information that we collect through our senses: It gets shunted off to some corner of the brain without our being consciously aware of it. We can train ourselves to be more aware of our environment, a "better observer," but still the vast majority of sensory information is treated to the same fate as the Ark of the Covenant in the first

Indiana Jones movie, forever lost among so many other moments of sensory input. Who decided to keep this information "secret" from your awareness, your conscious mind? The same entity that rolled the Ark away and into that vast warehouse... the Government.

Only, for our mind, "the Government" is the unconscious mind. The unconscious processes an enormous amount of information every second and stores it away. "Processing," in this case, means that the information is associated with other, similar, bits of information and other information that may be linked to it, given relationship markers to help determine its meaning, and finally a spot in the memory banks of our mind. Once it is tucked away, nice and comfy, it can be used to make new associations and meaning for both past and future bits of sensory data.

The same handling procedure is done to "ideas." Thoughts that we had in the past are treated to similar treatment and we can access them in much the same way as memories of past sensory information.

We say, *"past"* information, but the truth is it usually isn't much more than a half second old, if that much. We often treat the conscious and unconscious mind as if they were two separate rooms where mental activities go on separate from one another. When, in fact, it's more like a little room within a giant room. The giant room is our unconscious and the little, itty bitty room is the conscious mind. The little room gets all of its information from the big room. The manager of the big room [our unconscious mind] gets to decide what goes into the little room [which is managed by the conscious mind].

Why the two-chambered system? you might ask. Because there is no way the conscious mind can manage all that enormous amount of information in the same way the unconscious mind can. The conscious mind manipulates information [thinks] rationally. Please note: This is not to say that we are always "rational" and "ordered" thinkers. By "rational thinking," I mean that we consciously think in a way that uses information in an orderly and, most of the time, in a very linear manner. A good analogy would be an assembly line with one main conveyer belt stretching from one end of the itty bitty room to the other with small flaps at each end. Information gets fed in one end and slides out the other. Of course, where the information comes from is the great big room [managed by the unconscious mind] and the other end of the conveyer belt dumps back into a big pile which is also within the giant room.

This analogy is not to make fun of the rational mind. It plays an invaluable role in our very survival and the manner in which it handles the information that comes to it is much more detail oriented than the way it is handled by the unconscious mind. But we must remember that exactly what gets into that little room is controlled by the manager of the giant room, the Unconscious mind.

For the most part, there isn't a lot of direct communication from the conscious to the unconscious mind. There is *some* but it's kind of like a letter written by the conscious mind that gets sent to a translator who then puts it into something like a thought-enigma-machine [the Enigma machine was a coding device used by the Nazis during World War II]. The "message" then is coded and sent to the translator for the manager of the unconscious mind in the other room. That translator then decodes it into the language of the unconscious mind [the manager of the room], who then decides what is to be done. Remember now, the manager of that great big room is still in the position of deciding what gets into the itty bitty room. Having a piece of mail from the conscious mind doesn't mean the unconscious mind has to respond to the request. Let's say the unconscious mind has just fed the conscious mind a mental picture of a horse because the language center has just received a conversation about horses. The conscious mind hates dealing with vague and ill-defined mental pictures of horses, so it sends a requisition for more definition about the word that has been sent to the forebrain about a horse. The message says something like, "Hello there, oh Great and Powerful Un. How about a more complete picture of a horse down here. Something more suitable for conversation. I hate looking completely stupid in front of my mother-in-law, so give me something I can use to pull the wagon of this conversation a little better with, eh?. And, while you're at it, could you make the picture in something other than black and white? After all, we have a color TV and such, why can't we fill in our picture with something a little more interesting than *this* [see enclosed mental image]? --Rationally yours, The Conscious Mind."

The unconscious mind considers the message from the conscious mind [please note that the unconscious mind doesn't need the ego boost of capitalization of its descriptive title, unlike the rather childish rational mind] and, despite the not at all well-hidden snarkiness of the wording, decides to fill in color to the mental image [a rather nice shade of reddish-brown with some white patches] and also give it a large, sturdy body with oversized hooves and a hearty personality. "There now," says the unconscious, "that should help the conscious mind along and maybe give him a thirst for some Budweiser as well." And, as an afterthought [and because the conscious mind isn't the only one that can get snarky], the unconscious mind sends along a quick side thought of a horse letting loose with a sizable and decidedly smelly horse-bomb just to keep the conscious mind in his place.

All fantasy aside, the majority of the communications between the big room and the little room are not that complicated. And this little story is very inaccurate when it comes to what the unconscious mind is saying or thinking. That is because the unconscious mind doesn't think in a rational way. Rationality is how the conscious mind handles information, but it isn't the way the unconscious mind does it. After all, if the unconscious tried handling a gazillion bits of information every second using the comparatively slow and linear method known as rationality, it's very likely we'd be dead literally before we knew it! Remember that the unconscious mind has to manipulate not only a bucket full of information every instant but it has to give it associations and relationships and file it where it can be found again and decide whether the conscious mind might need it right away or even at all and, if it does, it has to put it into the queue so it can get translated into rationality before it hits that little door into the little room. And it all has to happen in a microsecond! [Whew!] Fortunately, there exists an information handling system that can do all this for an enormous load of data. It's called symbolism.

[4]
Symbols

Almost everything and anything can be a symbol. Generally speaking, symbols are stand-ins for real things. However, what constitutes reality is a bit elusive and has been cause for great debate in philosophical circles [as opposed to *real* circles]. If you look in a dictionary, you'll usually find the definition: "A symbol is something that servers as a representation of something else." For instance, in a dream, a chair could be a representative or symbol of something common, something sedentary, a general representation of furniture, a device that was used to mark the place you were to stay if you were naughty, a support for a weakness, any number of odd associations.

Dreams are saturated with symbols. That is why there are countless publications purporting to interpret your dreams. And none of them are very useful for the simple reason that we can't really remember our dreams on a conscious level without destroying most of the symbols. We can't for the simple reason that dreams are saturated with complex symbols. And to consciously remember dreams, we handle them as if they were rational thoughts... which they definitely are not. When we try to translate the dream into a story, we strip it of most of its meaning. Complex symbols contain a thousand-fold greater meaning than what can be captured with our rational thoughts. We can barely handle the simplest of symbols without getting mired in the ambiguity of symbolism.

One way of classifying symbols is to split them into three categories: logos, icons, and archetypes. There are other ways to classify and try to understand symbols but this simple three-way grouping works nicely for our purposes. However, many symbols can function in more than one of these categories and sometimes do so at the same time.

The most important information about symbols is that they are the "operating language" of the unconscious. In computers, an operating language is the set of commands that are referenced by programs to make the computer do what we want it to do. For instance, in the computer language DoDo2 [this is just a fictional example, you understand], the symbol that appears on the keyboard as "&" might be the command for *delete the last half hours' worth of typing*. Hopefully, you wouldn't strike that key. And, hopefully, that command would not be something you would put into the command structure of the operating language, let alone use in a program. But if it were, whenever your program came across the "&" symbol, it would wipe out the last thirty minutes' worth of work. Bad program; no cookie.

Symbols are the programming language of the unconscious. Our sensory information is converted into symbolism for information handling by the unconscious. It's easy to make thousands of relationships from one symbol to another and for it to contain thousands of associative pieces of information. That means information is given *meaning* when it enters the unconscious. In fact, *all* meaning is attached to a piece of information as part of its entry into the unconscious mind. Since we know that *all* sensory data enters the unconscious mind *before* it can enter the conscious mind, then the meaning of everything we think about on a conscious level is already determined by the unconscious mind. M*eaning* is the byproduct of the information handling process of the unconscious mind. It is the reason our conscious mind comes up with the meaning of the ideas we have without us having to dig into some mental dictionary all the time. It's the reason we "know" what our thoughts mean, even if our words sometimes fail us.

The *meaning* of our universe is entirely a product of our unconscious mind. This is an extremely important concept. In fact, it is the key to why and how we do rituals.

If we design a ritual that can add *new* meaning to a symbol or set of symbols, then we can change the meaning of those symbols or ones related to them. And that means we can change the meaning of the world around us. This can be done in much the same way as we normally do rational thinking but relies heavily on clever and careful use of symbols. The plan is to change the use of

14

a symbol slightly so that when the conscious thought is done [and slides back into the unconscious through the "dump" door of our itty bitty room] and becomes part of the information processing of the unconscious once again [remember, the unconscious mind will re-file all of what gets dumped] then the new information becomes part of the new meaning of the universe.

By the way, this is the same mechanism behind shamanic states of consciousness. And the same thing happens in hallucinations caused by drugs and/or severe physical stress. Such extreme techniques demand that the person must be extensively trained and prepared. Usually, when used for spiritual purposes, the "preparations" include rituals that can be among the most secret within a tradition. That is for the safety of the participants as well as a way to discourage unauthorized use of the drugs or stresses put on the people who make such mental journeys.

This technique for changing the meaning of our universe is not something solely used by ritual. It doesn't take much observation to see how the arts are sometimes able to change an entire population [poetry, music, dance, graphic art, even movies and TV]. Advertising is another form of the same technique. All of these are called *art* and often they don't do a very good job of changing much. But occasionally one will really stand out. One piece of music or a picture, even a breathtaking dance can cause many people to have an experience that changes their lives.

In ritual, the symbols used amongst the other experiences of the rite will go back into the unconscious and *add* to the meaning associated with that symbol and all of its relatives. We cannot erase the meaning already associated with the symbols but we can add to them sufficiently to make the old meaning ineffective. Some rituals are repeated because it may take several iterations of the experiences before the message can be sufficiently changed. The more senses involved in the ritual experiences, the more intense that addition will be, and therefore the more effective.

Two of the most useful senses for ritual are sight and smell. Sight because we tend to believe everything we see, even if our rational [conscious] mind doesn't trust it [and this is where sleight-

15

of-hand and stage magic got their beginnings]. And smell because we can't help but smell things [we *have* to keep breathing!], even though we quickly become consciously unaware of scents that linger for a long time. Some sounds, especially sounds without clashing harmonics and non-verbal sounds [so it doesn't have to go through our language center] can also be useful for such activities. In some cases verbal sounds such as nonsense words or words in another language unfamiliar to the listener can be useful because they confuse the language center enough to keep it from producing subconscious commentary about what else is going on. Combined with tone and rhythm, this becomes a chant that can quickly put a person into a light trance, thus enhancing the flow of information back into the unconscious mind.

By now, it should be clear that symbols are the main ingredients in rituals. They're what make the ritual work. But before we take a closer look at the mechanisms of ritual, we need to understand more about symbols so we can use them intelligently. We are going to look at three types of symbols but it is important to remember that what makes these three types distinguishable doesn't always apply to each symbol equally or even consistently to any given symbol. When using symbols to send a message back to the unconscious, we have to be sensitive to the many variables within each symbol. Some of these variables are produced by the individual personalities and acculturations of the people who participate in the ritual. This is an important factor in both the audience as well as the presenters of the rite.

Understand that the meaning of a ritual isn't going to be the same for everybody. In fact, it will be different in some way for each individual. Symbols are interpreted quite differently from one person to the next and often it is the attitude of the presenter(s) that can make or break the ritual having the desired effect. When writing a ritual, especially one that may be performed by many different companies of presenters, I will also usually write a commentary wherein I discuss the reasons for the rite and suggestions about how the ritual performers should present the ritual. Sharing the vision will help to give everyone a better experience.

[5]

More About Symbols

Symbols are simply substitution codes… this symbol means that; that symbol means this. The words written on this page are symbols for words we speak in our language. The letters that form the words on this page are symbols for sounds we make when speaking our language. And even the words we speak in our language are symbols for the meaning of our communications. As you study symbols, you begin to realize that almost our entire existence is filled with them. We have symbols that are substitutes for symbols that are substitutes for symbols that are yet again substitutes for some real thing. Our lives are filled with symbols and we can't even relate to our world without symbols being part of that relationship. Designing a ritual to make a specific change requires us to be very exacting in our use of symbols.

Of course, we want to be careful in our use of words. Words are the most common form of communication between people. If we were to write "dog" instead of "god," the meaning would be different. The two words are symbols that are very different from one another. However, the *letters* are symbols as well and, in this example, the letters are the same, only their order is different. By changing the order of those three symbols [the letters] we can completely change the meaning of our communication.

When I was very young [about 3 or 4 years old], I didn't know how to read or write. In fact, I had just begun to communicate through language. My vocabulary was very small and limited. A lot of the adult conversations around me didn't make much sense because I simply didn't understand the words or how the order of the words was supposed to make sense. It took many years of experience with the language before I could use it to communicate reasonably well. As my understanding of words and sentence construction grew more sophisticated, so too did my understanding of the world around me. However, my mental abilities were already capable of knowing and dealing with a very complicated world. The set of symbols we call language is extensive and the rules for putting words together in sentences are difficult. Much of our education deals with language symbols and the rules that govern them. Fortunately, our brains are well suited to learning and using language and it seems our skills in this area are much greater than any other animal's. But words are only a small part of the vast world of symbols and to become skilled in the use of symbols used within ritual requires constant study and practice.

Punctuation marks in written language have a tremendous impact on the meaning of the words. Not only do we have to get the words ordered correctly to communicate our meaning, we also have to punctuate those words correctly. "Don't... stop it!" if punctuated differently becomes, "Don't stop it."

Subtle nuances in how the symbols in a ritual are presented can change the meaning that gets transported to the unconscious. These nuances are very important, just as punctuation marks are for written sentences. Learning the "rules" governing them takes a great deal of time and energy of the person designated to write a ritual as well as those who present it.

One thing that can help you get a sense for these "rules" is mythology. Myths, folklore, fairy tales and the like provide us with what amounts to an encyclopedia of how a culture's symbols provide deep, hidden meaning that we can use for our rituals.

It's sometimes difficult to know how a symbol should or should not be used. Part of your decision should be based on how the symbol will function within the context of the ritual. Since nearly everything can be a symbol, we need to look at two important attributes that vary between symbols. Those factors are the *flexibility* and *strength* of its meaning. The more flexibility of meaning a symbol has, the less strength it has and vice-versa. For example, if you were to introduce a knife as a symbol, it could be interpreted as meaning a cutting implement, a weapon, a symbol of adulthood, a sacred object, a tool, or many other possibilities. It is quite flexible as a symbol and might require some context or explanation to fix its meaning within a ritual. That context might be from other symbols connected to it, a verbal explanation [but then, words are symbols as well], or a demonstration of its use within the ritual. A statue of a goddess figure, on the other hand, would be less flexible in its meaning. But it would have greater strength in its symbolic use over a wide range of people and cultures. Some things are extremely inflexible in their meaning but are extremely powerful. Using them within a ritual can give it great power but their use must be very carefully controlled. They have the ability to overpower all the other symbols in the ritual.

Logos – The most flexible type of symbol is called a logo. Our world is filled with logos, though their power of meaning is quite weak. There is, however, a gigantic number of them in everything we experience and their small power adds up quickly. The letters we use to make words are logos. The words themselves, whether spoken or printed, are logos. This entire book is made up of practically nothing but logos. But remember that a logo can have its meaning changed by something as small as the tone of our voice. And we can easily change the meaning of a logo by putting it in a different grouping of logos.

If we were to take only word logos and try to figure out what their meaning was, we would have to supply many possible meanings depending on the context. That is what a dictionary does and why there are often so many ways a word is defined. Even knowing all the different ways the dictionary defines it often won't cover some of the more subtle meanings for the word, especially if it is the kind that depends on non-verbal attachments such as facial expressions, hand gestures, body language, or physical surroundings. All of these things make logos highly flexible but also add degrees of ambiguity to their meaning. Still, logos remain the workhorse of nearly every form of communication and it would be impossible to interact with other people without the liberal use of logos.

You can easily change what a logo means, what it "stands for." They are the most mutable of symbols. Examples of this abound in language and elsewhere. This is a strength because you can use logos in almost any situation. But it is also a problem because no logo has a single, exact meaning and its use can be cause for some confusion. In any ritual you create, logos will undoubtedly have numerical domination but they will play a supportive role only. They don't have the psychological impact necessary to make sufficient changes in the unconscious mind. Because they are very weak, their ability to influence anything of importance is quite limited. You might think you could be overcome this problem by using more logos. But that tactic can backfire because people tend to get bored and cease paying attention after a certain point. Consider a long, drawn out lecture filled with words [which are logos] but no exciting focus. Yeah, you [and probably several others] in the audience fell asleep. If you were creating a chant that was intended to put people into a trance, this might be a useful method. Using sound logos, whether they make sense or not, can indeed produce a trance state if they are short "sentences" and repeated many times. But, normally, we don't want to put our audience asleep. Therefore, we need to dig a little deeper into the use of symbols.

Icons – An iconic symbol is less flexible in its meaning and use but it has a much greater psychological impact than a logo. That is, it's packed with more meaning with less ambiguity. There are considerably fewer icons than logos, but they pack a punch strong enough to change the unconscious associative patterns.

An excellent example of this is Coca Cola. Back in the early 20th century, the makers of Coke decided on an advertising program that has made the words, "Coca Cola," along with the fancy calligraphic swirls and intense red background into icons. Right after the Great Depression, Americans wanted to get out and travel the millions of back road miles that had been carved into the beautiful countryside of the nation. Because it was so far between towns in a lot of areas, the "Mom and Pop" or all-in-one store dotted the landscape in every non-incorporated part of the country. Of course, if you own a store, you need a sign so passersby don't think that ramshackle pile of boards isn't just some abandoned cabin. But fancy signs cost money and mom & pop didn't have much.

Along come the people of Coca Cola. They tell mom and pop that they will pay most of the cost for a big fancy sign if they can put their name, "Coca Cola," at the bottom. Of course, that means the store has to have Coke for sale and they'll even sell them a special cooler for half price to keep it all cold for the travelers that might have a thirst.

And so, all across the land on roads and back roads everywhere, the signs that had the fancy white letters and red background at the bottom became the sign of cold refreshment. Everywhere you drove, "Coca Cola" was what you saw. Coca Cola, Coca Cola, Coca Cola. You couldn't get away from it. The brand name became an *icon* of American road traveling with cool refreshment along the way. Now, our eyes only need to register the distinctive white on red fancy calligraphy and we know what we're looking at before we even sweep our eyes across the letters to read "Coca Cola." We could identify that sign even if we saw only a small portion of it, so strong is the *meaning* of that iconic symbol.

It is admittedly difficult at times to determine if a symbol is a logo or an icon. It's more a matter of degree in many cases. But the psychological impact of an icon should be the test. If the symbol seems to need other symbols to establish its meaning, then it is probably just a logo. But if it has an intenseness and high degree of established meaning, it is more likely to be an icon. This isn't an absolute test, but should make it easier in most cases to know what you're dealing with.

Archetypes – it was the famous psychiatrist, Carl Jung, who made the term, "archetype" well known as a descriptive of a symbol that is nearly universally understood to stand for a particular group of feelings and information surrounding a word or concept. There are many archetypical symbols and their use in rituals is often as part of the focus of the ritual.

Archetypes are the master symbols. They 'contain' an enormous amount of meaning which is nearly universal to all cultures and times. Although different cultures will put their own personal touch to these symbols, the bulk of their meaning is

22

shared with all humans. Quite a few of these symbols are paired with their 'shadow' symbol. For instance, Father is paired with Mother [I'm using capitals here to denote that these are archetypes] and God is paired with Devil. With very few exceptions, God is not paired with Goddess simply because they both represent such similar meanings. [The exception usually only occurs when the persons using and/or hearing the two words as significantly different are part of a spiritual group that worships both.] Hero would be paired with Villain and Fool would be paired with Hierophant.

Not all archetype symbols are part of a pair, nor do they require the other half of their pair to be utilized for symbolic meaning. For instance, the Hero can exist as a concept/symbol with or without the use of a Villain. But such dualities are a very useful way to generate energy, so it's helpful to consider the "shadow" of any archetype used.

Use of archetype symbols within a ritual should be done very judiciously since they are extremely powerful. Using more than one archetype in a ritual is risky and it's usually wise if it can be avoided. This isn't a hard and fast rule, but it is a good precaution. If a second archetype is to be used, it is better if it is the 'shadow' archetype within a pairing because there is less psychic conflict in the unconscious over the two coexisting in the same story.

Every ritual is basically a story. Stories inform us about worlds we aren't physically involved with but provide us with vicarious experience and information that offer new insights and meaning for us. To maximize the intake of these stories, rituals make the stories exist within specially designed environments that streamline our ability to reach and influence the unconscious mind. Many of the steps in the construction of a ritual are there to make this special environment. And like all environments, special or not, it's all a matter of perception.

23

[6]
Theatre of the Mind

There are two principles of magic that play an important role in rituals, both in how to construct them and how they work. First though, let's be clear on one thing: *All* rituals are for changing our reality. That might sound rather lofty but consider that the same thing could be accurately said about just about anything that facilitates a change. For instance, Aspirin is for changing our reality. Of course, the statement about ritual says it's for changing our reality and Aspirin just makes our headache go away. But what's the difference? Reality, after all, is strictly subjective.

So-called "objective reality" is a theoretical term, something that exists only as a mental construct like the square root of minus one. Everything we call "reality" is nothing more than mental activity. *If* objective reality exists, we would never know it because the instant we did, it would become subjective.

When we are down in the dumps, filled with sadness and feelings of existential angst [I've been wanting to use that phrase for months; doesn't it sound more impressive than saying "depression"?], our world is colorless, tasteless, and generally pretty useless. When we are in a happy mood, just the opposite is true. Is there a "happy pill" that can make our depressed world into a happy world? There might be, but it probably has a warning on the container that urges that you should speak to your doctor if your eyeballs start to bleed. Of course, there are other ways you could change your sad world to a happy world. For instance, you could go to a comedy club with a few of your buddies, watch clips of George Carlin on You Tube, or hundreds of other activities that could change your outlook on the world.

Because, after all, how we view the world around us depends on us, our perspective, our attitude. And what that world is like will change when our mental and emotional state changes.

Now, back to those two principles of magic; what are they?

    1. Everything is connected.

... and,

2. Perception is reality.

Modern physics seems to be proving that ancient metaphysics was right. For instance, one avenue of exploration currently going on in physics is about something called *entanglement*. These are experiments that seem to prove that what happens to an atomic particle *here* can produce changes in another atomic particle *there*... *instantly*... even when *here* and *there* are light years apart! So far, there are a lot of theories about this phenomenon but not a lot that make much sense except to just shrug and say, "Everything's connected." And then, of course, there's Mr. Schrödinger's famous cat. Dead or alive, the cat proves that our perceptions rule our reality. Our perceptions can be fooled and manipulated by events that depend entirely on our mental state. We can consciously decide to change our attitude.

We can change our surroundings and say that *they* changed our attitude, but that isn't entirely true. *We* decided to respond to the cartoon or fireworks or our lover in a certain way. To say that outside circumstances *made* us change is to give them way too much credit. We could have ignored them. Or we could have interpreted them differently. Ever try to cheer somebody up by telling a joke and watch it fall flat as they glowered at you with a combined expression of semi-pity and bored loathing? The *mind* changes the attitude when it damn well feels like it... period.

Rituals don't really change the mind but they do change the message that goes to the mind. By putting it in high-order symbolic form, the story told by a ritual has a great deal more influence than if it were just casually arranged logo symbols. That influence gets in the unconscious mind where the *meaning* of everything is formed. That influence can be enhanced by repetition [such as "Just call 1-800-IMA-FOOL. That's 1-800-IMA-FOOL. 1-800-IMA-FOOL. While supplies last, dial 1-800-IMA-FOOL. Operators are standing by. Just dial 1-800-IMA-FOOL to receive your free mystery package. (Just pay shipping and handling.) That's 1-800-IMA-FOOL. 1-800-IMA-FOOL. 1-800-IMA-FOOL."] [Don't you just love those? The problem is, they work!]

25

Does any of this remind you of Coca Cola, Coca Cola, Coca Cola?

Repetition is one way to raise a simple logo symbol and make it an iconic symbol. The negative side to this is that you chance boring or irritating the person experiencing that repetition. Another way of raising the status of a logo is to place it within a highly stimulating experience. This can be almost anything as long as the timing is correct. This is the basis of much sex magic. While the body is undergoing an orgasm, the mind is directed momentarily to the concept that is the target of the magic. [Please note: Sex magic requires a great deal of control, so be sure to practice, practice, practice.] Inclusion or proximity to other highly charged iconic or even archetypical symbols is also a way of raising the influence of a simple logo to that of an icon.

Remember that the whole purpose of elevating the status of a logo to that of an icon is to heighten its ability to influence the meaning of something in the unconscious mind. It is but one mechanism used by ritual to change the [subjective] reality base of the unconscious. This reality is what the unconscious mind uses to judge relationships and assign associative patterns to the information coming in from our sensory apparatus as well as the thoughts being fed back to it from the conscious mind. In effect, this reality base line is the relational database of the entire thing we call "thinking." It undergoes change all the time but only a little of that change is directed by the conscious mind. Nevertheless, we can consciously change this database in many ways, so we can truthfully say that we can consciously change our reality.

Knowing that we are making this change doesn't lessen the effectiveness of the ritual we use to do it. In fact, it makes it somewhat easier because we then have less fear about what is going on. But knowing that we *can* do this and knowing *how* to do it effectively are two different things.

As mentioned several times already, ritual construction is an art. Though you can be taught all about paint and brushes and canvas and line and color and, and, and... nothing teaches you how to paint as well as painting. Sometimes, even when you are mindful

26

of all that you've learned, you don't turn out very good art. Other times, when you don't pay attention to any of the techniques you've worked hard to learn, you produce a masterpiece. There are very few 'rules' about *any* art that have not been broken by masters of that art.

[7]
Lights, Camera, Action!

Creating a ritual is in many ways like creating a play, but don't let that lead you to believe it isn't serious business. Spiritual rituals can be life changing events for either good or ill and anyone who does not take constructing and/or presenting them as a sacred responsibility should not be doing the job. If you are involved in creating a religious ritual, you must never forget that you are wielding a powerful tool that can harm just as easily as help people. If that doesn't give you reason to pause and reflect, perhaps you aren't the right person for the job.

A story in a book is different than a story in a play. A story in a movie is different from a story in a stage play or book. And a story around a campfire will be different from any of those mentioned above. Why are they different? For one thing, they are played out in different environments and with different capabilities for relating the story. So each story must make use of the tools and capabilities of each of those situations. The way the story is presented will also depend on who is presenting it and maybe who is producing it. All of these considerations will also make a difference in what words and actions will be presented to communicate the story. Most of the time, spiritual rituals are designed and written by one or two people. How they are produced, how they are made manifest and presented to those who attend them, is often the work of several people with a director at the helm. This chain of activity and the roles of the people involved in the processes doesn't change much from one venue to another even if the titles of those people might be different.

Most spiritual/religious rituals are done from a script. A script differs from a regular story in two very significant ways. First, a script will name who is speaking and what sort of action should be happening on stage while the story unfolds. It is the speaking and acting plan for each of the actors. Second, a script will often give more exacting information and direction when the writer feels it is necessary to impart the motivations and intentions behind the words and actions described in the script. Sometimes, this will be in the form of a commentary that is sort of an explanation more for the director's benefit than for the actors'.

If you've ever seen a movie script, you will notice one thing right away: There is never any question as to who is supposed to be saying the lines [even when more than one person is speaking at the same time], and, with few exceptions, the staging and props are described in detail. In other words, there's little left to chance. Exactly what format is used for the script can differ from one to the next. But the format of the script will be consistent from start to finish.

Because revisions can happen at any time and it's the job of the continuity department to keep it all straight, script changes are churned out by the ream every day during the filming of a movie. It is a daunting but necessary task for such big productions. Fortunately, writing a script for a spiritual ritual is usually not nearly so big a job. However, it is in many ways a far more serious one. Whatever format you end up using, be sure that you are consistent so that those who must use that script know what you had in mind when you wrote it.

Here is part of an imaginary ritual script to illustrate one way it can be done:

HPS   *[Hands the broom from under the central altar to Maiden]*
"Clear this space of unwanted energies so we may make it sacred and fit for magic."

MDN   *[Begins sweeping widdershins, saying...]*
"Energy wicked or evil be,
Away from here, in haste do flee.
If not in accord with me,
Be gone bad spirits, so mote it be!"
    [Switches direction and sweeps deosil, saying...]
"Red spirits and black, white spirits and grey,

Come ye, come ye, come who may.
Around and about, Through in and throughout,
The good come in and the ill KEEP OUT!"
   [Everyone stamps their feet and says, "Keep out" along
with the Maiden]

Who is speaking, stage directions, and scripted words are all clearly shown so the presenters can be sure of what they are supposed to be doing. Obviously, writing a ritual in this manner is not the way to keep it a secret rite where you have to know what was done and who said a particular line before you could reproduce it. Such rites do exist. And, for whatever reason they are supposed to remain secret, this is not the format to use.

However, most rituals in these times do not need to be kept secret. So using a format that spells out what is to be said, who is supposed to say it, and what is to happen when the lines are delivered makes it far easier to conduct the rite properly. It also makes it better for the person in charge of directing the ritual. Rehearsals move more smoothly when such information is clear. Everyone has their own way of preparing for a ritual, but I strongly recommend serious rehearsals.

Two other tips you might want to explore: Modern word processing programs allow you to line number your text. This might seem unnecessary and maybe even overkill in some cases, but I've found it very handy for rehearsal scripts to be turned out this way. If you're in the director's seat, it helps to be able to say, "Let's go back to line 423 and read to 659, please." And last but not least, NUMBER YOUR PAGES! If you've got 10 pages that dropped on the floor after you pulled out the corner staple, you'll never question why I put that in all caps.

One last consideration concerning creating and conducting a ritual; spiritual rituals put people through changes. You've constructed a ritual that successfully does this, so what happens to the people who present it? What happens to those presenters when they rehearse it? For that matter, what happens to *you* while you are writing it and making changes in it? Any time you are creating any part of a ritual or doing a rehearsal, you are going to go through the changes the rite is designed to make. And the better you get at constructing rituals, the more powerful those changes will be. It might seem overdramatic, but PLEASE cast a protective circle while you are in the process of constructing your rituals or while you and your friends rehearse them. And don't forget to properly release the energies at the end of your writing session or rehearsal.

Creating, rehearsing, and presenting a spiritual ritual are magical acts, each deserving of special consideration and mindful focus. Anything less can and will produce undesirable results.

[8]

The Target

So, you're all suited up, the batter's in the box, and the umpire says, "Play ball!" It's time to start the game. Where do you throw the ball? Certainly not just anywhere, right? You've got to have a target or the whole thing is pointless. That is just as true with ritual as it is with baseball; without a clear goal, there is no reason to create or conduct a ritual. So, that is where we will begin. The first step in ritual construction is:

Decide upon a clear, understandable, and precise goal for the ritual.

This is absolutely the most important step in creating rituals. The better you get at making your intent clear, understandable, and precise, the better you will become at making rituals. [In fact, the better you will become at *all* magic.] This one thing will make your rituals either snap and crackle with power or fizzle and die, leaving everyone to wonder why they bothered to come.

This is not at an easy thing to do. You might *think* you know what your goal is and you could be completely wrong. As an example, what is the goal of a full moon ritual?

Most people would answer that the goal is to celebrate the full moon. Some might say it is to worship the mother goddess. Both could be said to be correct, but *what do they mean?* Exactly what is it we "celebrate" when we celebrate the full moon? What does the full moon mean to us? Are we moon worshipers? Do we believe that the moon would not rise unless we danced around, did some chants, and made all sorts of strange and mysterious signals? Oh, you say, the moon is just a symbol of the mother goddess? Okay, so what do you mean when you say, "worship?"

The better we understand our real target, the better and clearer our thinking becomes. If you can get the purpose of the rite boiled down to one simple sentence, telling what it is and why we want it a certain way, every other step in creating that ritual will come more easily and quickly. This is where I recommend you get in touch with your inner two-year-old.

By the time a toddler becomes physically able to roam about the world without having to be assisted, they start to learn there are rules to everything they want to do. The most important thing we teach them is that we make the rules and most everything their curiosity causes them to want to do is a no-no. By the age of two, they also have learned that there are *reasons* for a lot of the rules. Sometimes, knowing those reasons allows them to think around the rules. So, instead of saying, "NO!" all the time, they've learned to say, "Why?" In fact, "why" becomes their main fallback word for when they want to do something. By the age of two [or there about], they have become tiny politicians trying to find a way to get past the rules so they can get what they want. This is also the point at which their boundless curiosity about how the world works makes them into what all baby sitters call a pain the butt. "Why" become the chief investigative tool of the Terrible Twos. But "why" happens to help us get at the root of things better than nearly any other question.

Why do we celebrate the full moon? Why do we do certain things and call it worship? Why, why, why? For the moment, let's imagine a two year old has asked that first question of us:

"Why do you celebrate the full moon?"

"Because we want to mark that time each month."

"Why?"

"Because we recognize the full moon as a symbol of how special our mother goddess is."

"Why?"

"Because it happens every 28 days, like the menstrual cycle of a woman, which is the cycle that marks the reproductive time. It reminds us about how life is so special and how important women are in that magic."

By trying to explain things to a persistent inner two year old, we've arrived at a more significant layer of meaning and understanding of the event. This example might not be *your* understanding, and there is no reason mine should be considered better or "more true." But if you can't explain it any better than to say a full moon rite celebrates the full moon, you won't get very far creating a meaningful ritual.

Truly understanding the goal of a ritual is absolutely the most important part of constructing a ritual. If it is not done successfully, you will never be able to produce a ritual for it. Spend as much time on this step as you need because *everything* else depends on how deep your understanding goes. And a good test of how well you understand it is how short and precise your wording of it can be done.

If I were to try to boil down the goal I was attempting to explain to my inner two year old into one sentence, it might go something like this:

"A rite that links the full moon to the wonder of life and the magic of creation."

With that as my target, the result I want the ritual to achieve, I have already begun having ideas about what needs to be done.

[9]

Welcome to the Show

As with any project, writing a ritual is a complex task. Once you've refined the purpose, you have several other things to do before you can actually *do* the ritual. I have broken these down into eight steps and the last chapter was step #1. This chapter will be about the second step:

> **Establish the area that will be set aside for the ritual.**

This refers not only to the physical space but also the time, the people who will come to it, the people who will present it, and the mood and expectations of all of them. Whether you are doing this ritual for one or a thousand, the mood and expectations those people bring to the rite will play a significant role in how successful the rite will be. In a sense, you will need to set up *two* spaces for your ritual. You will need a physical space [and time] in which you will conduct the ritual, and you'll need to give serious consideration to the *psychic* space. Much of the time, at least in the modern Pagan culture, there is very little effort put into the mood and expectation people are going to bring to the rite and this will undoubtedly result in less than optimal energies at the event.

As any performer of any art will confirm, the attitude of the audience will always determine whether the event is a hit or a miss. Big name performers almost always pump their audience up with preliminary acts. That tactic also gives savvy performers information about their audience that will help them know how to play to the particular tone of that group. Of course, in a ritual, this would be vital information about how to better raise and focus energy as well as many other subtle tweaks that experienced ritualists learn to make when performing their art. So, making every effort to control the mood and expectations that are brought to the rite is just as important as being able to "read the audience" before you actually get up to perform your rite.

I've mentioned before about writing a commentary about the ritual after I've written the "finished" draft of the rite's script. The purpose of a commentary is to provide an in-depth treatise for the director and ritual presenters with the hope that they will have a more complete understanding of the ritual. Along with that, if you have ideas about how the mood and expectations of those who will be attending can be made more accommodating to the tone of the ritual, by all means put those ideas in there. If a particular time might be better than another, include your ideas and reasoning. Unless you wish it to be held secret, put down everything you think might pertain to the ritual.

Step #1 for creating rituals is in a class all its own. Nothing happens without it being completed. Step #2 [establishing the area for the ritual and the psychic energies that are brought there] is where you will actually have to start writing the ritual script. And, although you've possibly written down some notes to be included in the commentary about how the rite might be advertised, the actual script for beginning the ritual and letting everybody know that things are starting needs to be written. And make no mistake, first impressions are *very* important.

You have already decided on the purpose of your ritual. In all likelihood, you put that understanding to use in making announcements and/or posters advertising the rite. Not only did these posters, bulletins, or personal invitations tell when and where the rite would be but they also gave people a basic idea of the purpose. Now those same people are gathered at the doors or are wandering around, not yet really a cohesive unit of psychic energy. Your scripted words and actions have to now change them into a workable group mind capable of powerful magic.

There are many different ways the area can be established. You can hold the ritual in a special room, such as a chapel or temple area of some kind. Or you can "draw a circle" with a wand, athame, or sword. Perhaps you might use a circle of flower petals or salt poured on the ground or chalk used to mark the boundary of the work area. Any of these can work. Exactly how you make it known what the limits of the space are is up to you. But never forget that *everything* in your ritual must somehow serve the purpose you so carefully worked out in Step #1 [with the help of your inner two year old]. Whatever method and props you use to establish the area shouldn't fight the meaning of the ritual's purpose.

This shouldn't be difficult to figure out. If you were hosting a birthday party, this step would include the invitations, the decorations, and perhaps silly party hats given to the guests when they enter. Whether you're casting a circle or welcoming people into a sacred temple space, the way of it should simple and straight forward. A lot of traditions have standardized this part and made it easy to start your ritual with the words, symbols, and actions being almost carved in stone. Just be sure that they don't conflict with the purpose of the ritual and everything should be fine. However, you still need to write this part down and give the ritual presenters all the information they will need to handle this part of the ritual correctly.

I would like to add a side note here: Not every "step" in constructing a ritual is going to happen in an ordered and clear cut way. Some actions can have more than one function or fulfill more than one step. Also, some steps will have more than one activity designed to fulfill them. And some things that are included in a ritual might not really be part of one of the steps outlined here. It might just be something added in to make the ritual seem to flow more smoothly or just because it's fun or pretty.

Steps 2 through 4 are what I would term "housekeeping" functions. These steps exist to get everything ready to do the real work of the ritual, the magic that is designed to fulfill the purpose. They are the things that must be attended to so that everyone who attends the rite can enjoy its results.

Step #2 is essentially split in two. One part is about what needs to be done *before* everyone arrives [advertising, invitations, decorations, rehearsals, logistics] and what needs to be done *after* they arrive. Once it is decided that the ritual will begin, the script is what dictates what happens, what is said, and who says or does things. Every religious ritual I've ever attended had some sort of symbolic way of beginning the service. More often than not, this was part of the liturgical tradition of that faith or at least of that group.

Having some way to get everybody to settle down and begin to focus on the business at hand is necessary for every group activity. Using traditional words and familiar activities that signal the start of the rite works very well in most cases. This also makes writing the beginning part of the ritual very easy. However, tempting though it may be to just rubber stamp this step and move onto the next, be aware that every second of a ritual should be working to accomplish the goal you worked hard to refine and fully understand in Step #1. If you can use the opening moments to somehow strengthen the psychic connections between the participants and the goal of the ritual, do so. I would caution you not to stray too far from tradition, but don't be afraid to try new things, especially if they come as "inspirations" to your thoughts about the rite. More often than not, such flashes of creative thought are your unconscious giving you clues about how best to speak to it.

If you are just starting out trying to create rituals, you should be aware of a phenomenon that occurs to almost everybody at some point. Because ritual making demands that we try to achieve better communication between our conscious and unconscious minds, you can liken it to building a better communication highway for your phone or computer. Only in this case, that highway improves itself with more use. The more you attempt to become open to "hearing" thoughts from the unconscious [even though these thoughts are not in rational form], the easier it is to receive more of them. It's like the highway automatically expands with use. And our ability to "talk back" to our unconscious expands as well. We learn better ways to communicate in both directions.

This growth in our abilities most certainly helps us create better rituals because we can more readily produce beautiful and meaningful [even though they may not be rational] words and actions. However, there is a phenomenon that happens to most people who begin to expand this communication highway. I call it the "rush hour syndrome."

Halfway through the 20th century, America had recovered from the Depression, WW II and the Korean War, and was in a time of wonderful economic growth. One of the things that was a true testament to the great optimism of the country's population was the design of our automobiles. It was the '50's and the end of the small, stubby designs that had characterized the early half of the century's auto industry. Our cars became big, bold, and brash expressions of our freedom and our wealth. No longer was the family car merely a transportation device, now it had to make a statement about our status and that statement had to be louder and more grand than our neighbors'. To say that America had a love affair with our automobiles would be an understatement.

Along with the growing size and number of cars [it was at this time the two-car garage became almost a standard of new homes], America's road system was growing as well. Freeways crisscrossed the country and the highways that existed between cities and outlying developments grew wider and easier to travel. The time it took to travel twenty miles from work to home became less and less because of the better roads.

But the dream of the open road quickly turned into the nightmare of that ironic misnomer, "rush hour." No matter how wide the road and better the surface, all those cars that belonged to all those people who had been lured to the dream of a home in the burbs made that 20 minute drive to-and-from into a smog producing, fender crunching, headachy hour-and-a-half long test of human patience.

There are two other phenomena that are related to the rush hour syndrome. They too have to do with overcrowding, both cause [human nature] and effect [a ton of "stuff"].

The first is a theory about closet space. It says that no matter how big or how many closets you have, you will eventually find them all overcrowded. The second is similar but concerns altars. I warn my neophytes about this and they always laugh and promise they won't let it happen. But they do. The theory states that no matter how many or how big the altar, you will eventually fill them to overflowing with trinkets and remembrances. And I happen to think the same theory could, at least for most Pagans I know, apply to bookshelves. So, how does this pertain to ritual and the ever expanding flow of information between the unconscious and the conscious mind? Let's look at how the information gets from one to the other.

Information in the unconscious is handled through a system called symbology. Information in the conscious mind is in the form we call rationality. Both of these have their advantages and disadvantages but work well as long as they keep to their respective systems. Symbology is extremely useful for handling enormous amounts of information and being able to store it along with associative references and meaning, all within milliseconds of receiving it from our various senses and thinking processes. Rationality provides a sense of time and orderliness to small bits of information that are fed to us from the unconscious. This system allows us to survive quite well in a complex universe. But the information that the unconscious mind feeds to the conscious mind, and vise-versa, needs to be translated from symbology to rationality and back again. Otherwise, it's just gibberish.

It would seem obvious that there is some mechanism of the mind that "translates" information from symbology to rationality and back again. Normally, this works quite well. One instance where it doesn't quite measure up is our dreams. Ever notice that as soon as you try to consciously recall a dream it quickly grows fuzzy? This is because most dreams are raw unconscious thinking expressed in symbology. As soon as we try to explain them, we start putting them in terms of rationality where they quickly start dropping meaning like a maple tree losing its leaves in October. What we are left with is just a skeleton of meaning without the richness of color and fullness of meaning.

This "translator" is a busy guy, he never rests, and normally does a decent job. Now, because you are creating and doing more rituals, the communication highway begins to grow. More information comes and goes through the office of the translator.

The number of messengers from the unconscious streaming into his office has doubled what it was before you started this ritual creation business and it doesn't look like they're going to go back to their previous numbers. Not only that, but the messengers from the conscious mind are also increasing in number! The paperwork is enormous and things start to get a little messy. Sometimes, information from one mind doesn't get translated well or, gods forbid, at all! Raw, untreated symbology gets delivered to the conscious mind and you start to find it really hard to understand what is going on! Tiny rational thoughts creep out the door into the unconscious and cause havoc with all sorts of activities.

You start to question the meaning of everything and wonder if you can trust your thinking. You have a feeling of detachment from reality and the world that you once felt comfortably a part of.

You begin to suspect that you are losing your mind!

If all this sounds like I'm overdramatizing it, you're right. Except, in some cases, all these symptoms are likely to manifest in varying degrees. Knowing that this will happen at some point will hopefully keep you from spending a bunch of bucks at your friendly psychiatrist. You've been forewarned that something like these symptoms probably will appear, so just take a deep breath and settle in with a nice cup of tea and maybe a session in the hot tub. The good news is the symptoms will go away... eventually.

In the meantime, you've got a ritual to write.

[10]

Did Anybody Remember the Can Opener?

My father was a True Believer when it came to the All-American-Road-Trip. I grew up learning how to play the American version of Tetris; we called it "packing the car." When everything was ready, we'd all get in the family car and we'd go around the block twice. This was to give everybody one more chance to think of what it was we hadn't packed that we were *sure* we'd need. Most of the time, we didn't have to go back and get anything so the double circling of the block became more symbolic than anything else. After a while, it seemed that the road trip couldn't *officially* begin until we'd gone around the block twice.

There are some symbolic acts that may seem unnecessary but still should happen within a ritual. They're included because they represent a proper frame of mind or that everything that should have been done has been attended to. Step #3 is like that. The ritual probably could survive without it but it wouldn't *feel* right. [And how it *feels* is what it *means*.]

Consecrate everything and everybody in the area.

To consecrate something is to dedicate it to some purpose. You already know the purpose of the ritual, so what does it mean to consecrate everything and everybody? It means you take a final look [sort of like twice around the block] at everything you've put inside your ritual space and double check that each article, each tool, each image is in the right place and the right condition for the purpose of the ritual. Once you have done that, you might wish to symbolically bless or sanctify certain key items in front of the people so they can be sure everything is as it should be and that the presenters are paying close attention to the magical and spiritual wellbeing of them and the space they are in.

It is also a good idea to put some kind of consecration act in the rite that covers the *people* who have been kind enough to attend. This could be something as brief as a simple, "Welcome to

42

our rite," at the entrance or going around the circle, smudging them with sage or some other product with purification properties. Whatever you do or say, be sure that you accomplish two things with your act: First, you'll need to make each person feel that their presence is appreciated and that they are accepted as an integral part of the ritual. And you need to insure that whatever you do is at least not counter to the purpose of the ritual. If you can think of something that somehow corresponds to the purpose, so much the better.

Common actions used by Pagans that come under Step #3 are:

- Calling the Quarters, Elements, Rulers of the Watchtowers and the like.
- Smudging, asperging, or anointing of each person as they enter the circle or after the area has had its boundaries set.
- Giving some verbal or physical acknowledgement of how special the person is.

As mentioned before, some activities cover more than one step. For instance, is sweeping with the besom [broom] a way to establish the ritual area or to consecrate it? Yes to both. Taking a few moments to make one final check of all you're going to work with just makes sense. A smooth and orderly rite depends on how well each part, each tool, each meaning is known and understood by all. Taking a few moments to review everything you have brought to the rite and insuring that it is ready to be used in the proper manner will make it possible to give the people who attend the very best chance of enjoying the ritual's goal. When you construct the ritual, make sure that you provide a spot where the ritual presenters can do this. And be sure that the attendees know that is what is happening. It will give them a better sense of security and assurance that the presenters are doing everything they can to fulfill their duties.

Obviously, to consecrate something or someone is an act of will and generally doesn't demand any sort of corresponding physical action. However, it might be wise to use some gesture and/or words to indicate that the consecration is happening. This way, the people attending the rite will have a sign that the act of will is being performed.

As ritual presenters, the physical sign should not be ignored but it is much less important than the act of will. To simply go around the circle making a sign over everything is *not* what it's all about. The truly important aspect is what goes on inside the mind and heart of the ritual presenter *while* the gesture is happening. Keeping your focus on the object that is being consecrated and relating the *meaning* of that object with the spiritual ideals it represents requires a great deal of training. This, in fact, is the true test of a presenter's skills and qualifications. Almost anyone can learn lines and take stage directions, but only those who really *care* enough to give their time and energy in sufficient quantity will become a qualified presenter for the ritual sacraments.

Just as in the example of using a broom to sweep the area, several other customary ritual activities will serve multiple functions. Whether we are talking about Wiccan circles or Baptist services, there will always be activities that are traditional to that faith group that serve more than one purpose. This is especially true of activities that fall within the first four steps of ritual construction as outlined in this work. Because of that, the order in which some of these steps fall will not be the order in which they are discussed here. It's also true that one step can be covered in multiple ways within the same rite. There's nothing wrong with this and, in fact, it's often a good idea. Sometimes, saying or doing something one way won't convey its meaning to everyone, but finding some other way of giving that message might just work a lot better for those who didn't catch it the first time. And, especially for the next step, providing a second way to relate to the meaning might help even those who understood your first method of communicating it.

[11]

So... What Was the Question?

This is the last of the 'housekeeping' steps. By now, I'm sure you're tired of me saying that the first step is by far the most important one in the whole process of creating a ritual and that every other step depends on what you've set as your goal. In some ways, this might seem obvious but perhaps it is *too* obvious because so many people don't bother figuring out exactly what the goal of their rite should be. And then they wonder why it was so bland and failed to do much of *anything*. So, yeah, putting a lot of thought into what the goal should be is mighty important. But communicating that goal to everyone who attends the ritual is almost *as* important. It doesn't do much good to put all that thought into the purpose of the ritual, dealing with that annoying inner two year old and trying to wrangle with the wording, boiling your thoughts down to their essence of *meaning* unless you can communicate that message to everyone that comes to your rite.

In all likelihood, you have configured your ritual so that its purpose is pretty clear to everyone before they show up. You have, so to speak, primed the pump. This does something very positive because it helps insure that only people who are interested in the goal of the rite show up and that they come with the expectation of that goal happening. Both factors will aid the presenters when it comes time to raise the energy. But, just to be *sure* that everyone is on the same page, there's one more step you need to accomplish: *Crystallize the vision.*

If I sat you down beside me and we both viewed a beautiful sunset, we both would have experienced almost exactly the same thing but it would quite probably mean something different to each of us. Not different enough to matter much in most cases, but perhaps enough that the meaning would affect our associations with the event later on. However, if we also heard an especially beautiful poem about a sunset shared by two lovers, the likelihood of us both having more congruent ideas about the whole thing would go up quite a bit. Similarly, if we both watched a TV documentary about the sun, we might be better educated about it but would that sunset have the same meaning to each of us? Hardly. There's an important message here: **Information and meaning are two very different things.**

The process you went through to complete Step #1 was for getting at the core *meaning* of your ritual. That little conversation with the inner two year old wasn't just to be cute. It was to get you to think about what your vision *meant*. And using that "inner two year old" model was purposely offered as a little bit annoying and a little bit comedic for a very good reason: It opened up your connections to your feelings. And why is that important? Yep: **How it feels is what it means.** It's a lot easier to understand the purpose of your ritual when you can *feel* it.

That is how you're going to fulfill Step #4. You are going to get everyone to *feel* the purpose. Although you might have to dig a little, do some research, this actually is rather easy. Once you know the meaning of the ritual, you know what the feeling is you will want to communicate. There are several ways for you to communicate that feeling. However, they all will require a certain artistic talent.

Beautiful works of art take tremendous talent to create. But to display or in some way to communicate that art requires a sensitivity to not only that particular media but also to the people who will be observing that art. Creating good ritual is an art and presenting one is another sort of art. In all likelihood, the presenters of your ritual will be more skilled at presenting words than they will at, say, dance. You might find a dance that you think perfectly conveys the feeling you have determined portrays the purpose of your ritual but can you expect it to be presented by the folks who will be up there in front of the crowd trying to crystallize the vision so the ritual can proceed?

When scripts are written for big movies, the script writer doesn't have to worry about who is going to present the story on screen. That will be the producer's job. And the writer really doesn't have to worry too much about how the script will be interpreted by the actors; that's the director's job. Similarly, it's the screen writer's job to switch up things so every camera angle is covered correctly and all the special effects are produced for the right scenes, etc. In fact, for large budget movies, there are literally *thousands* of jobs that must be done before the popcorn gets sold.

But you, my friend, don't have the zillions of dollars and thousands of skilled workers at your command to construct your ritual. In all probability, you don't have anybody else who can help you craft a ritual. And, even if you did, ritual by committee is most often too much like a platypus.

Finding something to help those who attend your ritual *feel* the essential meaning of your rite isn't rocket science. As I stated earlier, you already know the right feeling, all you need to do is find something that will create that feeling for the maximum number of people. Whenever I've run into a problem doing this, it has *always* been because of one thing I was doing wrong: I was *thinking* about it too much... with my *rational* mind. Don't be concerned if the *information* about the purpose is not contained within whatever you choose to create the *feeling*. You can always use words to reiterate the goal. But, by producing the right feeling, you will transform the *meaning* of those words so that the people will be aligned with your vision of what the results of your ritual should be.

There are many ways to combine feeling and information. Songs, chants, even a short bit of instruction about keeping a focus on certain key points while engaging in some activity can work. Responsive readings, poems, a particularly moving bit of text, even a joke can do this. If done artfully, this step and the next one can be so complimentary, people won't feel anything except a smooth ride from one step to the next.

Which is just fine, because the next step is where the magic begins.

[12]

Throw... The... Third... Switch!

I apologize for the title of this chapter. I just couldn't help myself. It is, of course, the famous line Dr. Frankenstein said to his assistant when he wanted to zap his 'creation' and bring it to life. It's also the line delivered by Gene Wilder to Marty Feldman in the modern spoof movie, *Young Frankenstein*. In any case, it was the command to begin the process the good doctor had prepared for. And the next phase, Step #5, is all about finally getting your vision manifested.

Raise the energy.

Of all the steps in constructing a ritual, this undoubtedly is the most misunderstood. To truly know how to "raise the energy," you have to first comprehend what is meant by the term, "energy."

We almost always describe energy in terms of how we wish to use it or in how we measure it. We describe a light bulb in terms of how much light it produces. For incandescent bulbs, we would often use the wattage used by the bulb to indicated how bright it was. With the production of the CFL, LCD, and several other light bulbs now on the market, it's gotten harder to know exactly how much illumination you can expect from a light bulb. You can find the amount of *lumens* a bulb puts out on the packaging now and that helps, but most people aren't that familiar with the numbers to know what they're getting.

For the moment, let's take a look at how the energy is measured. We'll go "backwards" from the light we use to see with. First, there's the *lumens*, the standard measurement of the amount of light the bulb puts out. That is powered by the electrical energy, the *watts*. The electricity is powered by a complex system of machinery that uses quite a few different possible sources for its energy. There are hydroelectric generators, coal burning electrical plants, wind, tidal, solar, thermonuclear; the list goes on and on. Each of them have been used to produce the energy we call illumination. And yet, none of them are raw electrical energy or light [oops, solar power *is* light, but we turn it into electrical energy to power our light bulbs]. Hydro-electrical energy is actually not produced by water [hydro] but by gravity [water *falling* over fancy turbine wheels]. But gravity isn't light. Those turbines turn shafts that move *magnets* around and they produce electricity. But magnets aren't light either.

Are all of these things energy? Actually, you could say they are, but they really are just ways we use to describe how we experience the energy. The light we use to read by is powered by the gravity that moves the water that turns the magnets that push the electrons that heat the gas or filament in the bulb and it glows. So perhaps we should describe our light bulb in terms of how much gravity it takes. But, you say, that wouldn't make much sense. No, it wouldn't. But the energy seems to change names depending on how we are trying to handle it. Surely the energy that makes things visible to us doesn't change as much as we change the way we are describing what it does to the things we use to handle the energy. Isn't there some way to just describe energy without having to use some sort of device to handle it in some way? And if there is, how would we then describe that energy?

Yes, there is. And when I tell you what it is, you will realize that you already knew it. You will see why the way an electrician describes energy is the same as how a man using a couple of horses hitched to his plow describes energy. Why the frightening energy we call the atomic bomb is the same energy a baby uses to push a ball. And when a student of metaphysics talks about the energy of a thought, you will understand it is the same as when a physicist speaks of the energy of a black hole. Because energy is really only one thing and yet it is behind everything.

Energy is *change*.

Change powers the universe. It is the single constant of everything that is, was, and ever will be. All change takes place within two [or maybe it's really one] conditions: space and time. When space/time becomes different, we call it change and when we try to describe and measure that change, we call it energy.

Oh, and not to rain on the parade, but we don't produce energy. We may manipulate it, but we definitely don't produce it.

It takes energy to manipulate energy. And I just said *we* manipulate it. That implies that *we are energy*. That's right; we are. We are in a constant state of change. Which means we're in a constant state of energy. In fact, just like the rest of the entire universe, we are all energy. And when it comes time to "raise the energy," we will do it with our own bodies and minds.

Now do you see how dancing around in a circle or chanting nonsense words or drumming together can make the magic happen? No? Well, that's okay, it'll click here shortly.

Remember back when we were talking about making sure everybody who attended the ritual should be on the same page about the purpose? Remember that I said that if you were clever enough, people wouldn't even notice when Step #4 turned into Step #5? This is exactly how you would lead into raising the energy. Because getting everyone to the point where they *felt* the *meaning* of the purpose is the same as getting them to the beginning of raising the energy. It's only a matter of making an association between the purpose of the ritual and the manner of making some sort of obvious change.

Let's say you wanted to heal a boil on Ben's bum [if you are named Ben, sorry, but I *don't* mean you]. And let's assume everybody understood the purpose of your little get together. One way to raise the energy would be to have everyone turn to the right and clap their hands while chanting, "Ben's bum, Ben's bum, make the boil cut and run." And on the last word, they'd all stop clapping and slap the bum of the person in front of them.

All right, so it's silly. What did you expect, Robert Burns?

We'll talk about laughter in a second.

This chant, silly though it may be, fulfills all the points necessary to raise the energy:

1. It is simple and easy to learn.
2. It has a rhythm that will help get everyone in sync [in this case, both in sync with their breathing and very likely, with their heartbeat].

50

3. It has a solid mental association with the purpose of the rite.

Probably the easiest method of getting people "in sync," is a drum rhythm known as the "heart" beat. As the name implies, this mimics the sound of a heart. We all heard this sound for the first nine months of our existence on this plane; every part of us tuned to respond to this rhythm. You could think of it as the archetype of drumbeats. Unfortunately, the heart rhythm on a drum is rather limited to a small selection of purposes precisely for this reason. Everyone associates it with the pulse of life.

Whether we are talking about using a chant, a song [yes, there's a difference], a dance, some other kind of body movement, a mental and/or physical exercise, or some other action, raising the energy has to comply with numbers two and three and, in most cases, also with number one in the above list.

The exception to number one happens when a group of people has practiced a complex action enough they have mastered it as a group to the point where it doesn't occupy their conscious mind any longer. A good example of this would be the "Om" meditational practice. This is much more than a meaningless sound that gets repeated. Done properly, it will slow the heart and calm all bodily activities. Done as a group meditation, it will, much like the heart drumbeat, sync the breathing and expand the channel to the collective unconscious.

I have personally only witnessed one time that the use of "Om" was done correctly. Unlike the far too common use, which is something like, "We're going to chant Om for about a minute and a half and then we'll all believe we've done something magical," there was a remarkable change that was *felt* in the room after about seven or eight minutes of the monks chanting. It was like the room had separated from the rest of the world and that time was somehow different. Other changes took place but I'm not qualified to even try to describe them. I wasn't part of the group that was chanting and undoubtedly their experience was quite different from mine.

There are many complex methods designed to leave the everyday conscious world and commune with your inner self but none of them are easy or learned quickly. That doesn't mean they absolutely can't be used for ritual but they shouldn't be used in rituals for people who have not been schooled thoroughly in the correct techniques of using those methods. At best, improper use would lead to low results. At worst, it could be a major disaster. Admittedly, this would likely be a freak event, but it's possible that such a misuse of an inner-work method could throw some into a psychic misalignment.

I'm sure some might consider that warning as delusional or overly dramatic. But I have personally witnessed some very bad results of ill-considered ritual practices and caution you to take great care with the power you wield. Always consider that the energies you are trying to raise must come from the people at the ritual and they always will be an unknown factor. Having sensitive and knowledgeable presenters can help neutralize potential problems but you should fashion the method for raising the energy so that it can be done in small, well controlled increments. In other words, don't just open the floodgates and hope that nobody drowns.

Raising the energy under ritual circumstances requires that the activity you use for raising that energy makes a psychic connection with the purpose of the ritual. Usually, this is not difficult to do. Normally, telling everyone a little about how the energy raising activity relates to the purpose is sufficient. However, the people deserve at least a hint about how dancing around the circle, doing the Pagan version of the Bunny Hop, relates to celebrating the spring equinox. If the method for raising the energy makes sense to you, you should be sure it makes sense to the people attending the rite. Then again, if you can't make a sensible connection between the method for raising the energy and the purpose of the ritual, you definitely won't get the results you've hoped for.

Example: "All right, we're going to blow up these red balloons and bounce them around the room. That's because the red balloons look sort of like tomatoes. And tomatoes rhymes with potatoes. And the purpose of this rite is to grow potatoes."

Uh... okaaaayy. Well, that *might* work. But frankly, you should try to relate the activity to the purpose a bit better than that. But, even as silly and far-reaching as that "connection" is, I've seen far worse ritual energy raising where there was absolutely *no* connection made and it would have taken ten pages of logic to show any association at all.

The second condition listed was that the energy raising method should have a rhythm, a pattern that will help get everybody working together. Think of the work songs sung by field workers, chain gangs, and laborers around the world. They're used because they distract the conscious mind from thinking about how hard the work might be [or how menial, demeaning, or just plain horrid] and help mold everyone into a group mind. Once again, we're back to that common thread in all three conditions, getting beyond the conscious mind and the internal dialogue, as well as clearing the path for the symbology to reach deep into the unconscious and give new meaning [and therefore a new reality] to our world.

But raising the energy isn't quite enough to accomplish our purpose. The energy needs to get things done and our ritual has to form the energy into the right kind of magic so we can step back, confident that our magic will keep on working until our goal has been reached.

So the next step is how we manipulate the energy.

[13]

Three In One

Unless you plan to spend days [or longer] raising energy, you need to plan for when the presenters decide enough energy has been raised. When you're writing a ritual and you come to the part where you are raising the energy, it's probably best, after you have explained what the presenters are to do to raise said energy and how to tie it into the purpose of the ritual, to simply write directions to the presenter that go something like, "Work it until the energy is sufficient." That's because no two presentations of a ritual will ever be the same. What could take one minute of energy raising with one group might be ten minutes with another. This is where you've got to trust in the experience of the presenters. But you also should do everything you can to help them build and manipulate the best energy structure possible. So, step #6 in our ritual construction plan is:

Focus, direct, and release the energy.

Of course, this sounds like three different steps. Except they all connect to one another and each facet of this step can't operate without changing the other two. So, although we will discuss each part as if it were separate, keep in mind that they all are parts of one thing.

You might be wondering why this step doesn't also include raising the energy. Look at it this way: A simple example of raising energy would be like going over and turning up the thermostat. That action doesn't, in and of itself, make the room warmer. And just because we've turned up the dial, the only thing *we've* done is a very small act that *begins* the process of warming things up. If the thermostat isn't connected to a complex of very carefully constructed devices, our action definitely *won't* heat the room.

I have a little sign I printed out from somewhere on the internet a while back. It says, "Your energy flows where your focus goes."

54

I thought it was a rather clever way of saying something profound about magic, so I printed it out and hung it where I'd see it most every day. But actually, the saying is not *exactly* correct. In fact, how it is wrong points precisely to the problem a lot of folks have when they attempt to raise energy for a purpose: There is a difference between *focus* and *direction*.

I'm going to illustrate this using a model I happen to be very familiar with, optics. I grew up learning the optical trade from my father and light and lenses are an excellent way of showing how energy can be manipulated.

First, let's establish that although optics deals with some very specific forms of energy, the principals involved are analogous *for all forms of energy*. So let's see what we are using for our model:

The energy we will talk about is called *light*. In this case, we will just deal with the light that our eyes can see, the *visible spectrum*. We could just as easily use x-rays or radio waves because they too are part of the larger spectrum but we can't see them with our biological eyes.

The device we will use to demonstrate how we can manipulate our energy will be a *lens*. In this case, a clear glass lens will work nicely. Our eyes can see the light as it passes through the lens. If we were dealing with x-rays, our lens could be completely opaque to visible light but still manipulate the energies of our x-ray generator in the same way as the clear glass lens does for visible light. Lenses are created out of many different materials that use different physical properties to manipulate various forms of energy but the ability for them to focus, direct, and release energy is not so different in principal.

Most of the time, we speak about how a lens focusses light as if it was not connected to its ability to direct it. This, of course, is absurd because for the lens to focus light, it must focus it *somewhere*. But let's table that discussion for the moment. To focus the light, the lens uses the properties of its materials to bend the direction of the light that enters it on one side and makes it come out the other side of the lens at a different angle. Light passing through a lens will always bend toward the greater mass of the lens. So, if the greater mass of the lens is in the center, the light will bend toward the center as it passes through the lens. This will concentrate the light and make it come to a point at some point beyond the point it exits the lens [except when the lens is a sphere, then the light comes to a focus *inside* the lens]. If the lens is thinner in the middle than it is at the edges, the light will bend away from the center and disperse as it exits the lens.

This is important because this model can be used as an analogue for most aspects of manipulating magical energies. There is a third possibility for a lens. In this case, the lens is the exact same thickness all over. It will not bend the light that travels through it. In reality, such a lens is nearly impossible to produce without some flaw being detectable with our own eyes. All you have to do to see the flaw is to look at something through the glass and move your head from side to side while maintaining your gaze on the object. You will notice a "waviness" to the scene through the glass. Even very high quality windows have these flaws, though less so than the lower quality windows. *The lesson here is that it is almost impossible to pass energy through any lens without bending that energy in some way.* [By the way, this is exactly why the stars "twinkle." Our atmosphere is an imperfect lens.]

In magic, our lens is our will. In ritual magic, the lens is the *collective will* of the people who attend the ritual. And, like our glass lens, how we shape the lens will determine whether the energy is concentrated to a sharp point or dispersed widely.

One other property of our example lens needs to be mentioned here. All lenses filter the light that passes through them. In practical terms, this means that some of the light [energy] will be lost when it passes through the lens. This isn't a problem *if you have enough energy [light] to begin with*. In fact, sometimes it is a benefit. Take your standard sunglass lens for example. We *want* less light and maybe a selective color of light while out in the sun. And, of course, filtering out the UV rays is also helpful. Our eyes don't see the UV rays, but they can damage our eyes and sunglasses that filter them out are better than ones that don't.

Just like our imaginary glass lens, what happens to the energy that passes through our magical lens will be influenced and governed by the makeup of the lens and the shape. The "material" of our magical lens for our ritual is the ritual presenters, the ritual itself, and the people who attend the ritual. And, as mentioned, the shape of our magical lens is the collective will of all the people while they are raising the energy. Your ritual script and the talent of the presenters can influence that collective will. But remember that the people who attend the rite will have a big part in that collective will and your talents as well as the talents of the ritual presenters must lead the attendees so the energy is formed correctly.

The sign I got off the internet would perhaps have been better if it said, "The energy flows where the *attention* goes." I happen to wear glasses; I'm what you'd call blind without them. And when I'm not wearing them, when the lenses aren't directing the light into my eyes, I'm pretty useless. Believe me, if the energy [light] isn't directed correctly in your ritual, the purpose of the ritual won't happen and you'll feel pretty useless too.

If my purpose was to make the room warmer and I got up, went over to the wall and flipped the light switch instead of the thermostat switch, I would have performed the same energy raising process but with the wrong direction of the energy.

Xlffh, K szxy/g bkrkyb uh vkybdfx gnd fkbng ckfdgklyx. Sorry, I wasn't giving my fingers the right directions.

In the previous chapter, it was mentioned that there should be some kind of connection between the purpose of the ritual and the energy raising process. But this alone doesn't insure that the energy has been given the right direction. For instance, if the purpose of the ritual was to heal Ben's bum [you mean it *still* needs help!?] [just work with me here], then we could do the clap hands, chant, and slap the bottom of the person ahead of us. The relationship between the purpose of the rite and the energy raising process in this instance is relatively easy to see. But, it is questionable as to what direction all that energy is supposed to go.

If you were to do this ritual, you wouldn't be able to direct the energy because you don't know Ben [or his bum]. But, if I were

57

to give you a picture of Ben [just Ben, not his... well, you know], you would then have a direction to send the energy. Or, maybe the energy could be directed to be associated with a special coin or a piece of jewelry that would later be worn by Ben. This is called a talisman or an amulet, depending on whether it is carried [talisman] or worn [amulet]. Two special cases to this are the genie [energy contained in a vessel] and the icon [energy imbued into a piece of statuary or other image, such as a photograph].

Of course, as with most magical energies, it is the mental [psychic] handling, the associations between the energy and the target that make the difference between success and failure. This is the main reason that magic on demand [which usually starts by somebody saying, "Okay, you're so magical, do a spell to prove it."] is nearly impossible. Under such a challenge, your mind is focused on *proving* something rather than the discipline and will that is necessary to accomplish the magic. All spell craft [and rituals are definitely a form of spell craft] takes time to achieve the desired goal. And having to instantly produce some sort of "proof" is totally disruptive to the processes of magic.

Deciding where the energy is to be directed is only part of the story. Actually making the energy go in the direction it's supposed to is the other half of the equation. This requires the ritual's presenters to be skilled in what is known as *stage presence*.

The truth is, there isn't much you can write into the script for your ritual that will provide this skill. But it is important that you don't put in stage directions or words that will get in the way of the presenters while they are directing the energy. Once again, you'll have to count on the sensitivities and abilities of the ritual presenters. You can put down your ideas and suggestions in the ritual script itself or the commentaries, but be sure to let them know that you are expecting them to be aware and thoughtful leaders for the people they serve.

Being a ritual presenter is a demanding job and experience and training are necessary to become the right person in charge of a ritual presentation. No amount of talent in constructing a ritual will ever cover up for bad leadership during its presentation. Think of it this way: You can write like Shakespeare, but if the actors are bad or the director is not good enough, the play can fall on its face.

However, it is also true that knowing how a ritual works and how all the elements of its construction operate can be a great help when actually producing and presenting a ritual. And, if you are a ritual presenter, a good actor *can* make a bad script sound better!

Being sensitive to the mood and feelings of your audience is vital when you are a presenter but knowing how to sway the hearts and minds of the audience is vital to constructing good ritual as well. Remember that the purpose of the ritual will always be to change some part of the universe for those who attend. The way to do that is to speak to the unconscious and add meaning to the associations the unconscious ascribes to certain circumstances. And *meaning* depends on *feelings*.

Each step in constructing the ritual requires an understanding of human nature, an awareness of how words and actions can affect how people feel. But none rely so much on the experience and sensitivity of the presenters as much as this step. Everything you've produced so far has led up to this vital step and it will ultimately depend on people you might not even know. They will be *there* and you are only *here*. But if you have been a ritual presenter and experienced the connection between presenter and audience, you can better understand how to write a ritual that captures the heart of an audience and moves their mind and soul.

The last part of this step is to *release* the energy. Going back to our analogy of a lens and light, this would be where the light has passed through the lens and is now leaving it. It's obvious that the lens can no longer affect the light. Nor should it; if the lens were once again introduced to the light, all the focusing and directing of the light would be seriously changed. No, let the energy alone, free to do its thing. [Shine on, little sunbeam, shine on! It almost sounds like a children's song.]

Oh, that more ritual presenters and audiences followed this advice.

Releasing the energy means to let it go, to let it do the work it was designated to do, the purpose of the ritual. To hang onto that energy in any way is to change it, subvert it, spoil it. But I constantly see two large mistakes being made concerning this step. The first is a mistake on the part of the presenters [and maybe even the ritual's writer... don't let this be *you*]. It has to do with either ineffectual leadership or not knowing what to do. The other is on the part of the attendees to the rite.

Imagine an orchestra without a conductor. Somewhere after the second note, utter chaos breaks out. That's the same reason a ritual presenter is needed for raising the energy. Now imagine the conductor up in front but just turning his back at the last measure of the piece being played. *That* is a lot like what happens at a ritual where the process for raising the energy is not "turned off" clearly and cleanly. Instead, it just sort of fizzles to a ragged and very ugly end. When this happens, the energy is almost useless and everybody feels let down and tired. When the energy is raised to an appropriate level and then crisply stopped with everyone understanding that it is to be ended at *that moment*, people don't feel tired and the energy is in a nice, easy-to-be-used form.

This doesn't mean the chanting or dancing or whatever else you might use for raising the energy is always abruptly ended. It's possible for it to gently fade or end in some other fashion. But it *does* end on cue and everybody stops trying to make more energy at a well-defined point. Think of it in terms of the orchestra conductor. The music may end on a high note, a low note, a cymbal crash, a fading note, or even a cannon going off, but it ends when the conductor makes the final gesture and everybody stops playing music at that point. No second guessing, no competition to see if you can blow that note longer than the other guy, just end it **now**.

This happens only if the conductor does his job correctly. It isn't quite rocket science but it does take skill and paying attention to every part of the group you are directing. Conducting a ritual is much the same as conducting an orchestra when it comes time to raise the energy. The ritual presenter designated as the conductor of that portion of the ritual must be able to keep track of the energy and the people raising it. They need to be able to conduct the process so that...

   1. Everybody stays coordinated and working together
      and...
   2. He or she [the conductor] is aware of the level of the energy and how much more he can get from the attendees without exhausting them
      and...
   3. The attendees are cognizant of the conductor's control and in agreement with it.

If all three of these conditions happen, the conductor still needs one other skill: They must be able to know when the energy is slightly more than sufficient. That is when it needs to end.

Why do we need slightly more energy than what would be considered sufficient for the magic to work? Simple: you don't throw a ball so it stops at the catcher's glove, right?

Ending the energy raising activity doesn't end how the energy is used. Proper direction to the goal of the ritual does require two more things. Those are the last two steps of ritual construction.

[14]

Step #7

Every energy system has some device for handling excess energy production. Dams have spillways, electrical systems have fuses, and magic will always need a way to...

Ground the stray energy.

In the previous chapter, we learned how to utilize the magical energy produced during a ritual. Remember to always produce more than you would use to accomplish the goal of the ritual. What you do with the excess and why you must include that as part of the steps to ritual construction also tie in with that other thing that is often done wrong with the energy of the ritual by those who attend it. Truly grounding the stray energy means more than just putting the energy where it won't hurt somebody, it also means to let go of the energy... *all* of the magical energy. Although this is really very easy to do, many rituals fail to include it as part of the ritual and suffer for the inattention.

Ritual is purely a mental or psychic activity. In constructing it, you have created a place, time, and condition outside of the physical plane in which the energies that have been generated will help change the world of those who have attended your rite. You have done what you can to make these people feel safe and comfortable in that psychic realm and you now need to close up shop and trust that the magic will work.

Because it *will* work. All that energy produced by all those carefully directed people with all those well-crafted symbolic messages can't help but do some real magic. The only thing that could go wrong would be if somebody deliberately went in and did some psychic messing with your hard work. Somebody like that motor-mouth over there who just *has* to rehash the ritual, talk about the energy raising, and try to second guess the magic. Somebody who wants to immediately critique the ritual because they think it should have been this or that, blah, blah, blah. Yeah, somebody like that.

We can't help but go over *in our minds* a ritual we've just been a part of. In fact, the ritual would not have any chance of working if we weren't affected in that way. However, rehashing what was done and why it was done that way is like putting your hand into the middle of the pie after it's baked. It will make it into a mess.

Proper circle etiquette says that talking about the ritual anytime soon after doing it is a big, bad no-no. Period. And, in most cases, "soon" means within one moon cycle. It's okay to turn to your neighbor and say, "Gee, that was fun," but that's about the most you should say. Yes, it may be natural for everyone to be *thinking* about what they've just experienced but conversations that cause everyone to hang onto the energy will always produce bad results.

It might be prudent to have one of the ritual presenters remind the attendees of this circle etiquette but it is also wise to take away the excess psychic energy as quickly after the end of the energy raising part as possible. This will make it far easier for people to calm down and turn their attention away from the ritual. In a sense, the ritual has ended and what the next two steps are designed to do could once again be called housekeeping.

Grounding the stray energy means finding a way to get rid of the excess psychic energy. Since getting everyone into "ritual mode" was important so the psychic energy could be raised and sent to do its intended purpose, Step #7 needs to reverse the whole thing and get everybody back into "normal" mode. The easiest way of doing this is to engage one or more of the physical senses. Eating comes to mind and it is a very good way get the mind back down to the mundane physical levels. It engages our vision, our sense of smell, taste, even touch. It's a very good way to start conversations [not about the ritual, though] and it also replaces some of the energy that the body has used up during the ritual.

Grounding is an important step and should never be missed after doing ritual. Otherwise, you will be sending a bunch of people out the door and maybe on the road while they're still not fully engaged in the here and now. That is, quite simply, irresponsible.

I know that a lot of traditions say you should ground yourself *before* going into ritual and that isn't a bad idea either. That gets rid of a lot of the things that could take your attention away from the magic that is to come. But grounding *after* the ritual is absolutely necessary. Write something into your ritual script that essentially says, "No matter what, ground the stray energy." If you have a suggestion about how this should be done, say so. But, once again, this could be left to ritual presenters *if they know how to accomplish it*. Unfortunately, not all ritual presenters are aware of the simple way to do this and, worse still, not all are inclined to recognize the need for it.

Many groups of Pagans hold potluck meals after circle is done and this too has the benefit of getting people in the right frame of mind to once again go out into the "normal" world and be fully aware and connected to it. However, before the circle is opened [un-cast], you need to do something to ground everyone, even if it takes just a minute. This doesn't need to be elaborate, anything that stimulates one or more of the physical senses will usually work. A small diversion from the psychic world at this point is critical, so don't forget it and don't let the ritual presenters forget it.

Once the stray energy has been grounded, there is only one thing left to do.

[15]

Du-Da, Du-Da, Du-Da, That's All, Folks

When you throw a birthday party, at the end you hand everyone their coats, thank them for coming, maybe send them on their way with some cake and a funny hat and close the door. Is it over? Nope. Because now you've got to clean the space you used and straighten up after the party. Because you will want to use the same space for other things. The same is true for your ritual. However, included in your list of things to shut down you should remember your guests. Not only do they need to ground their stray and excess psychic energy, but they also should be returned to their former condition. Of course, they won't be returned to the *exact* same condition as when they arrived [the magic will be influencing them as soon as it was released]. But the better you can eliminate the associations between the ritual and the mental and physical space used for the rite, the easier it will be to keep people from sticking their hands into the pie.

So the last step in ritual construction is:

Return the area and the people to their former condition.

Although most traditions have a standard formula for doing this, make sure the ritual you create has clear instructions for what is to be done to accomplish this final step. And I have found that it's a good idea to make a time for the ritual presenters to do an especially intense grounding after everything else has been shut down. I've come to use this grounding formula even after a rehearsal. In so doing, the presenters become used to the words and symbols that are used for the procedure and each time they do it they get better at visualizing the results and the magic works better. This speaks to the value of tradition and repetition in ritual and we will speak more on this in the next chapter. But having some sort of closing that is well known among many of the attendees of your ritual will really help to finalize the ceremony and provide a distance between the ritual and those who have been part of it.

It should be obvious why this step is necessary but apparently it wasn't so obvious to one group who put on a public ritual one time near my home. For some reason, they had a reputation for putting on good public rituals and I was in the middle of producing *The Spell of Making*, my other book about ritual construction I wrote back in the early '90's. I was just finishing up the chapter about Step #7 [grounding the stray energy] and was about to launch into the chapter on this step you are reading about now.

I went to the ritual. It was in celebration of Lammas and everyone brought some kind of food offering which they put on a couple of long tables near the spot where the circle was to be held. It was a perfect late summer day, sunny and warm with a gentle breeze and a few fluffy clouds making the sky dance with shapes that sparked the imagination. The day was a perfect setting for a magical time to be had by all.

The ritual was rather ho-hum and then it wasn't anything. The ritual presenters just up and walked off! Not even a goodbye! It took a good thirty seconds of bewildered silence before somebody said, "I guess that's it." Then everyone kind of wandered over to the tables and began filling their plates. It was the most dramatic lesson possible about why the end of the ritual should be clear and understood by all. The energy, what there was of it, was left to drag on the ground and scatter and the people were left hanging. I was more than disappointed; I was furious and left as soon as I could. I should have stayed and tried to patch up the mess as best as I could, but I was in no mood to be a priest at that point.

Good ritual form should be understood by everyone who creates and/or presents a ritual. Whether you are building a car or driving one, you need to know certain things about how cars function, the rules of the road, and where you're going. If not, problems are just waiting to happen. You should know when to stop and everybody else should also be notified that you are stopping. That's why they invented brake lights!

CRAFTING PAGAN RITUALS

There are countless examples of how the final two steps of ritual construction should be carried out but I will site one that I have done several times over the years. I call it the Go Fly a Kite spell. Mind you, there really is no distinction between a ritual and a spell except you usually do a spell by yourself and a ritual with others [the operative word here is, "usually"].

The setting can be a park, a field, the beach, or any other place where you can safely fly a kite. Have a good, strong line at least seven hundred feet or more long. It can be a box kite, a regular diamond kite, whatever you like. You also will have to prepare several slips of paper upon which you've written a worry or care that is bugging you. Only one worry per slip of paper.

Launch the kite and play out the line until you've got only a hundred feet or so left on the spool. Then, one by one, tie the line securely around each of the slips of paper. Allow at least a yard of line in between the worries. As you tie up the pieces of paper, say something about how you are done worrying about it and how you are sure that the gods will take care of it even though you are still willing to work on it. Just not willing to worry about it anymore.

When you've run out of slips of paper, things that worry you... cut the line. Immediately turn away and walk back to your car, *never looking back!!!* Drive away and go get a pizza or something.

I've performed this ritual, this spell several times. It works like... [wait for it...] *magic!* It also is the best example I can speak of concerning the importance of finalizing the ritual and *letting the magic do its thing*. It is always the right thing to do: Get out of the way and let the energy work as intended. And make sure the people who are a part of the magic sever their connection to the process we call ritual. Just cut the line and walk away.

67

[16]

Tradition

When you begin to write rituals, you usually think about only the ritual you are writing at that moment. Little if any thought is given to possible future rituals. But, as time goes on, armed with the understanding about the way ritual works and as the elements of constructing one become more clear to you, you will be called on to produce more rituals. This can be quite time consuming but there are some "tricks" you can use to make the process easier. One of these has to do with what is called a "tradition."

The word generally means a standardized way of doing something. Pagan traditions, sometimes just called, "Trads," refer to what other religions might call denominations. In Pagan traditions you have several categories of traditional things. You have what holidays are celebrated and their relationship to one another as well as their meaning within the spiritual philosophy of that tradition. You might have some significance to certain colors, emblems, symbols, even special gestures or art forms. You would definitely have some rituals that were shared across multiple groups and maybe some code of conduct or "laws."

What is called a *liturgy* is the collective written [or, in some cases, only oral] tradition of the group. Liturgy is more than just the rituals but they make up a large part of it. And one thing that helps a spiritual tradition is for the rituals to have some shared elements. Things like the same words said at the beginning or end of the service, or parts of each ritual that contain similar phrasing or concepts. Not only will this make it easier to learn the rituals but it will also make it easier for those who attend them to feel the emotional connections they are designed to create.

One thing that will help you if you have written a few rituals is what I call *modular* construction. This is like the modular home construction where you pick out the room designs from a large selection of possibilities and then there are a certain number of ways the rooms can fit together into a home. It makes for better construction in most cases and an amazing number of possible configurations.

Let's say you have written a set of Elemental invocations for a ritual. Each invocation has been worded to relate properties of the Element to the purpose of the ritual, which we'll say is to bless the start of the outreach education program of our coven. Perhaps we'll say the invocation for Air went like...

> Element of Air,
> Light and fair,
> Heed our call,
> Inspire us all.

It works out well for you and you are asked to create another ritual for some other purpose. This time, it's a healing ritual for...

That's right, Ben's bum. [Poor Ben. This has to be a chronic condition.]

Now you might use part of the invocation you wrote for the blessing but adapt it to something more suitable for a healing rite:

> Element of Air,
> Wind in the hair,
> Come to our aid
> With the Mother's care.

Okay, it's different in several ways. But it still has a similar feel as well as the advantage of being easy to come up with for an Elemental invocation. If you use this form for many more rituals, you will be forming a liturgy with your creative touch woven into it all. This will also make another thing possible: Good spontaneous ritual on demand.

My wife and I were once invited to a summer solstice rite many miles from our home. It was a beautiful drive and we arrived around noon at the rural farm that was hosting the ritual. After mingling for about two hours with others as they arrived, we approached the hostess and asked when the ritual was to begin. Her answer startled us.

"Oh, whenever you like."

It seems that one, teensy weensy detail had been omitted from our invitation. *We* were supposed to conduct the solstice ritual!

This was back in the early '80's and we would typically just pack our ritual gear into the trunk of the car and go. We had learned that it was smart to bring at least enough that we could, if necessary, loan out a couple of extra robes, candles, incense, and various other altar gear in case somebody forgot something. The box we usually kept this gear in even held some statuary and a broom and a sword. Even though we didn't know that we were supposed to lead the ritual, we were prepared.

Except, we hadn't written a ritual and didn't have one from a book with us. As my gym coach used to say, it was time to dribble back to first base and punt. Imagine the surprise we felt at our hostess' answer; imagine the panic.

Did we? Panic? Of course not.

Well, maybe a little, just for a moment... or two.

Then, as the comic books say, we sprang into action. [I'd always wanted to sprang.] We walked back to our automobile, opened the trunk and started pulling our gear.

With what we could carry in our hands [and a sword strung over my back], we told everybody to follow us as we marched toward the tree line that bordered the property. Mind you, we'd never been at this place before and had no idea what was in the woods. But we figured we'd find a suitable spot if we walked long enough.

We thrashed our way through the underbrush for maybe 10 minutes when we came upon a nearly perfect circle of low grass surrounded by magnificent evergreens, alder and maple trees. The circle was about twenty-five feet wide and had four large boulders at the edge, spaced almost perfectly for the direction altars.

See? The gods always provide what we need.

Even our hostess didn't know about this spot and she'd grown up on the property. She asked us how did *we* know where it was and we answered with a line we'd gotten from our initiators:

70

"We have our spies everywhere!" [That will always stop them from asking further.]

Neither my wife nor I had discussed what we would do or say for the ritual. Throughout the entire time from the moment we'd learned that we were expected to conduct the rite, we were busy getting gear and herding people into the woods. Then we were too busy trying to keep from falling into the blackberry bushes and avoiding nettles to plan anything. But we had led a coven through several years of full moons, new moons, and sabbats and both of us had a good idea of what needed to be done. We had our purpose: Conduct a summer solstice ritual to celebrate the longest day and the wonder of the sun god. At no time during all this had we discussed anything concerning the ritual.

But we knew how to *make* a ritual. We knew the eight steps to constructing *any* ritual and we had gotten us to Step #2 already without needing to even think about it. We emptied our arms of gear and began instructing a couple of helpers where we wanted things. Then we put on our robes. This was the right signal to the others and they began robing up as well. In about five minutes after we'd stumbled onto the circle in the woods, it had been made into a beautiful Pagan temple suitable for high magic.

And so, we began the rite. I don't remember what my wife and I said. I do remember that there wasn't any hesitation, no conflict over who was supposed to do or say which part, no stumbling over lines. It was completely off the cuff and natural. It was from the heart and it was magic. The gods not only had provided the perfect spot for our ritual, they provided the right words and actions.

The ritual lasted twenty or thirty minutes; I really don't know. Time changes when you're doing really natural magic. Afterwards, we shared some wine one of the people had carried along and sat and talked about summer things. Then we packed up and said our thanks to the gods by making sure the spot was thoroughly cleaned. And we began our trek back to our hostess's farm.

By the time we got back, we'd had received several compliments about the ritual we had "written" and about a dozen requests for "copies" of it. My wife and I didn't want to admit that we'd made it up on the spot, so we just smiled and told people we couldn't give them copies, it was private coven material [well, that was *kind of* true]. But from that day on, we *always* ask who is going to conduct the ritual when we are invited somewhere!

None of this could have happened without a knowledge of how rituals work and how to create one from the ground up. While the exact same thing happening to you is unlikely, it's quite possible you will find yourself the only one with the "right stuff" to take care of a magical need or problem. Also, there is an annoying idea from some quarters that rituals should be always be spontaneous and/or by consensus. While it's quite possible for good rituals to be spontaneous, it is highly improbable. This is because the principles and methods for employing them taught in this work are not widely understood. And this isn't just within the Pagan faith groups. Many religions don't even teach what rituals are for. Many consider their rituals to be hardly more than exercises in devotion and obedience [and *some* are just that]. Nearly all of the revealed religions consider everybody else's ritual to be *evil* and often won't even admit to having rituals in their own practices [an idea that would be laughable if it weren't so pathetic].

As for ritual by consensus, this too has a regrettably low chance of turning out well. I have worked with committees to develop rituals and it wasn't pretty. The idea looks good on paper, but the problem arises from human nature. Think about it; the idea of consensus is that everybody wrangles with the same problem, sharing ideas within the group until one idea finally emerges as the most proper and fit. Everybody agrees that idea has won the almost Darwinian process and they all go out with that as the decision of the group.

And butterflies can do brain surgery.

The reality is that the idea that benefits the strongest persuader will be the most likely winner. This is more true than we ever would like to admit but throughout history this has been true of all ideas from all groups. Any exceptions are probably lies told to others who weren't in the committee at the time.

I did work with another to produce a ritual once. It was a painful and difficult process because we both wanted to keep from dominating the decision process and try to see the viewpoint of the other. For creative works such as ritual, this is not an efficient way of doing things. We did, however, craft a ritual with good energies and some really beautiful parts in it. In fairness, I should mention that my wife and I [as exemplified by the story of the summer solstice ritual] have produced many very good rituals together but I don't count that as group work. She is fantastic at wording things into very good poetry [and, as you have already found out, I am not] and, other than some wrestling over what symbology might work best or who will be assigned what activity, we really do work as one. She and I have been magical partners for better than 30 years and knowing one another's mind began the day we met.

Most of us, when trying to do something new that we know very little about, feel it best if we have some kind of mentorship from somebody whose opinion in such matters we respect. This is perfectly understandable and ritual construction is certainly a complex and difficult an art as you might ever engage in. But it *is* an art. You would never learn how to paint if your mentor mixed the colors and held your hand while you did every brushstroke. And you can't expect that you'll learn to construct rituals if you constantly want your hand held for every word and magical act.

Instead, I recommend that you work in near solitude until you hit a spot that stumps you ["inspiration" usually comes in small packets and hitting a creative wall happens even to so-called experts], then feel free to ask anybody whose opinion you respect. But be careful, they likely won't have knowledge of the eight steps we've just covered and their suggestions and opinions may not be as good as yours, despite their experience and knowledge. Art, like beauty, is truly in the eye of the beholder.

And, speaking of beauty, at the beginning of this book is an acknowledgement page. On it, in big letters, you will see three words: *"**Beauty is Spirit**."* I want to expand on those three little words because their meaning have transformed my life. Don't worry, this all relates to ritual construction.

The idea of the four classical Elements making up the universe was old when Greek philosophers used them to help describe various aspects of their world. Nobody really knows where the concept first came along, but the "atoms" of the Greeks have come to mean pretty much what *they* meant by the word. They are the basic building blocks of the universe. Forget the fact that we've split the atoms of our ancestors into ever smaller pieces until we now refer to things such as strings, membranes, and even more exotic ideas about dimensions described by completely unimaginable mathematics. The notion that the universe consists of basic *things* which are part of everything in infinite combinations is pretty much how humans have looked at their world ever since Ralph fell out of the tree and broke the coconut into smaller pieces.

The physics of today is finding it hard to keep from treading into the realm of metaphysics. Many modern-day physicists are sounding more and more like ancient metaphysicists. They are right at the edge of being mystics and they're flailing to not tumble over the edge. Perhaps in another generation or two, physics will make magic into a science. In the meantime, I'd like to give you some food for thought:

A few systems of magic proclaim Spirit to be kind of the combination or the source of the four classical Elements. It is often referred to as "the fifth Element." Several years ago, after I'd written *the Spell of Making* [the book, not the spell itself], I kept having questions about Spirit. In the spell, Spirit is given a "position," [the center of the universe] and sort of an attribute [dwelling in the person at the center], but it didn't really give any description of what kind of things constituted its domain [like Air, Fire, Water, or Earth]. I went on a quest, a Spirit-ual quest.

I won't bore you with the details [I've written a book called *Be ALL!* about the details], but I've come to the conclusion that beauty is quite simply how we perceive Spirit, kind of like Spirit's "radiation." For all intents and purposes, beauty *is* Spirit. How does this relate to ritual construction? Like this: As in all art, some will see beauty and some won't. If *you* can see beauty in your work, you've connected to its Spirit. If others can see [feel, actually] beauty in your work, you've created a true spiritual sacrament. You can forget all the fancy analysis; if it's beautiful, you've done your work correctly.

That's not to say your ritual has necessarily fulfilled a particular purpose [Ben's bum might still be a problem], but it has fulfilled the greatest challenge of any priest or priestess, to pass on Spirit. Love beauty and you won't go wrong.

[17]

The Deep End

I have been to many beautiful spots in the world. There are so many in the USA it's impossible to pick just one and say it is the best. But in Washington State, there are more than enough to keep anyone in awe for several lifetimes. I was lucky enough to be born and raised in Washington and I'm thankful for that blessing every day. In the foothills leading up the west side of the Cascade mountain range, about 60 miles east and slightly north of Seattle, lies the tiny town of Index, Washington. It is spread along the north fork of the Snoqualmie River as it tumbles down from the mountains and heads for Puget Sound. Brave adventurers use its wonderful rough waters for white water rafting and residents and tourists alike pull trout and bass out of its waters during the summer. It's small wonder this area is loved by any nature loving, tree hugging, free spirited Pagan. And, just outside of Index there is a church known as the Aquarian Tabernacle Church. It was started back in the mid 70's by a fellow named Pete Pathfinder Davis, whom I am proud to call my friend.

The church [usually referred to as the ATC] has grown in influence in both local as well as national and international Pagan communities. By the late 80's, the ATC was holding regular monthly services up at Index. They were timed to be on the Saturday as close to the third day after the new moon as possible. This is commonly referred to as the Diana's Bow moon because the slim crescent of moon visible at this time just after sunset looks quite a bit like a Roman bow. It was hoped that holding a ritual each month at this time wouldn't interfere with the usual full moon celebrations conducted by the many small covens around the area. The ATC wanted to give the Pagan community a gathering place where many different traditions could meet, interact with one another and exchange ideas, build community and promote common values. To do this, Pete invited different groups to present a ritual for the Diana's Bow meeting each month. It was quite rare that the same rite would be done two months in a row or even two times in the same year. This gave the event a somewhat haphazard energy flow and people were often disinclined to travel 60+ miles for an unknown quality of ritual gathering. The church wanted to be a neutral place for newcomers to interact with the more establish Pagan community personalities but there wasn't much draw in the on-again-off-again quality of rituals that were presented.

I proposed a new strategy for the Diana's Bow ritual. I thought if we [the ATC and me] could develop a ritual that had a powerful message, combined with a well-trained troupe of ritual presenters, it would become well known throughout the area and draw Pagans new and old. I worked on my proposal and showed it to Pete. He liked it and I began writing the ritual.

I hadn't been working on it for more than a couple of weeks when an idea struck me. What if I wrote *two* rituals that were exactly alike in the beginning and end but had interlocking messages? Could I even do that? I hadn't ever seen such a thing before but I had seen whole traditions that used the same opening and closing as well as several other parts of their rituals which were the same from one rite to the next. I wanted each ritual to refer to the other so that no matter which one you saw first, you would be able to see the connection to it when you experienced the other one.

The more I thought of it, the better I liked the idea.

As always, before I got carried away in how to do something that ambitious, I first had to get the purpose of the rite straight in my mind. I knew the church needed something to attract new Pagans as well as something that would give more experienced ones a reason to come back. But I also had to tie it in with the time of Dianna's Bow [also referred to as, "DB"] and be sure it was relevant.

When I began this project, I hadn't written a ritual for the church before. In fact, I had only written rituals for our coven to present, some public and some private. However, I knew that presenting a ritual wasn't a job you handed to just anybody. People needed to be trained and rituals worked best if rehearsed. I began to look on the project as a possible training mechanism for future ritualists.

I eventually came up with a concise statement of purpose for the rite: A worship service for Dianna's Bow that focusses on *beginnings*. The entire script for the ritual(s) can be found in Appendix A. The script has line numbers because we're going to use it to analyze and show how each part relates to the eight steps you've learned.

[18]

Every Word Has Power

Although it isn't the goal or purpose of the ritual, there is an alternative statement about it that should be made about the reason for working on the ritual: *To produce a meaningful Diana's Bow ritual that would fulfill the spiritual needs of those new to the Neo-Pagan faith and motivate them to return the energy back to the church in whatever way they could, thereby causing the church to grow in scope and effectiveness.* Remember this as well as the shorter statement of purpose in the previous chapter. Both the purpose of the ritual and the reason for constructing it play into its form and function.

Now I would like for you to read over the ritual before we do any analysis of it. Go ahead and read it now and then come back to this page. But you might want to keep your finger in the pages in the appendix so you can look again at the line numbers as I refer to them.

THE LOOK OF IT

Before we analyze it line by line, let me point out a few characteristics of what you see. First, the entire ritual is written down in a format that makes it clear who is supposed to do and say what and where people should be standing or what they should be holding during the ritual. This format is what I mean when I say you should write a ritual as if it were a script. That essentially is what this format is like, a script. I could take this script and hand out copies to several people and say, "OK, Bob, you will take **NORTH**; Janet, you take **SOUTH;** Ralph, you're doing **HP**...," and everybody would be able to easily see what "parts" they would be doing. Most actions are spelled out on the script and very little is left assumed. While it may be argued that such a tight choreographing and staging makes it impossible for spontaneous feelings and actions to happen, I think that is quite simply not true. I've written hundreds of such scripts and no two rituals have ever been the same from any one of them. Each person lends a different tone to the parts and things just happen which cannot be predicted. You can do a ritual a hundred times and it will never be exactly the same.

Notice that speaking parts have a different look from stage directions. In this case, they are in bold face type and all caps. Also, quotation marks are around them with the exception of a few items such as the responsive reading under **CALL TO MYSTERY**, lines 347 through 386. How the ritual is written, the format, the use of different print styles and fonts, these all make it easier for the ritual presenters to understand what the ritual builder had in mind. The watchword here is **communication**. If you're going to take all that time creating a ritual, it makes sense to write it down in a fashion that conveys your vision of what the ritual should be like. Most of my rituals have a look similar to this example, though I've never set it in stone and play around a little bit in an attempt to find the "perfect" way of presenting a ritual in written form. I use a computer and word processing program, which makes all this infinitely easier.

Because this ritual is meant to be memorized, I have not done what is advisable to do for rituals that are to be read by candle light. For them, I produce the speaking parts in much larger size type so they are easier to read by the dim light. Frankly, I'm terrible at memorizing lines and I cheat and read them from a paper or note card most of the time. While this is probably never advisable if the lines **can** be memorized, I plead a horrible memory and pull out my script so I won't stammer like Porky Pig. It is advisable that a copy or two of the script be available even if everyone has done the ritual dozens of times. Nobody is so perfect they can't "choke" and forget a line.

A ritual of this length and complexity requires a great deal of rehearsal. The parts of **HPS**, **HP**, **MAIDEN**, and **WARDER** are long and complex. The directional or **QUARTER CALLERS** don't have nearly the number of speaking lines as the others since I conceived that their parts were to be given to people who were just starting out in presenting the ritual. And it was believed from the start that they **could** read their lines from note cards. If they showed ability in those roles, they could be considered for the role of **WARDER** or the **MAIDEN**. Their roles do require them to keep track of many things and to project certain attitudes during the rite. But they essentially have a lesser role in the ritual because those spots were purposely designed as entry points for any interested in playing a more important part in the ritual activities of the church. While it is desirable for them to rehearse, it certainly is not necessary for them to rehearse as intensely as the major players must.

Rehearsing brings to mind directing. As the author of your ritual, you really should think about directing the rehearsals and maybe even playing a part in the presentation of the ritual. Nothing will teach you more about how to improve your ritual making abilities than to do this. Just writing the ritual is not enough. You must have some way of finding out if it does as you have intended. If you act as director, you will have the opportunity to go over the ritual and find the areas that need to be changed. I guarantee that you will find things in a rehearsal that you never imagined while quietly sitting and writing the ritual. Going back and doing a rewrite is far more preferable than allowing something less than your best to be presented. Also, having a part in the presentation of the ritual will once again provide an opportunity for finding better ways of doing and saying things. And sometimes "accidents" can be inspiration for future ritual writing.

Every new perspective that you can experience concerning your ritual creations will add to your knowledge and instincts for building new or improving old ones. A good example of new perspective happened to me when I started writing this chapter. The ritual in Appendix A was written quite a while before this chapter was started. I hadn't read through it for several years until I was checking it over after importing it from my files on another disk to the appendix. I caught myself reading through the ritual as if I hadn't been the one who wrote it. It was an enlightening experience viewing my own creation as if it were somebody else's. I learned some new things about the ritual simply because of that change in perspective. Other people's reactions and thoughts

81

should be sought every step of the way. Feedback is your best tool for improving your abilities as a ritual builder. Actively seek it out and listen with an open mind.

There is not a ritual made that can't be improved in some way. Often you will be your own best/worst critic. In understanding the formulas and techniques of ritual construction, you have a rare and valuable knowledge that most of your critics will not have, but don't let that make you too smug to listen to your critics. Sometimes criticism that is not well focused can be helpful because of your knowledge. One of the best ways to improve a ritual is to go through it one sentence at a time and analyze it after you have written it all down, as we will be doing here. Always keep the goal of the ritual in mind while you read through the ritual and use it as your gauge for the suitability of every word and action. Think about how people will respond to what you have planned and always ask yourself if there is a better way to achieve the ritual's goal. Don't be afraid to write up an alternative ritual using something that has come to mind during your analysis. Compare the two and see which you like best afterwards and also pass around both of them to whomever you feel can give you the best feedback. Now we are going to analyze the Diana's Bow ritual that I've given as an example.

ANALYSIS

Step #1 in the process of creating a ritual is to get a solid understanding of the goal of the ritual. In this chapter and the one before, I've talked about the various reasons for writing the ritual and what it was supposed to accomplish. Then, in the ritual text itself (lines 7 - 17), you will note that the very first statements are designed to communicate those goals to the people who will be conducting the ritual. However, if you read my first account of the goals and the ritual text's statements, you will find quite a difference in wording and it might seem at first glance that I've changed the goals.

82

Actually, what I've done is to refine the original goal statement. It is now stated as two main "mysteries" that will be presented within the ritual and some subordinate ideas that are products of those "mysteries." The rest of the text (lines 19 - 109) before the **PURIFICATION OF THE CIRCLE** also supports the overall goals of the ritual and helps establish the attitude of those performing the rite.

Probably you are wondering why I use the word "mystery." It works like this: every ritual is designed to carry the participant through a symbolic experience whereby they can grow in spirit. Some experiences are labeled as "mysteries" because no two people will discover the same thing about their spirit from these experiences. The common link is that it is a spiritual discovery. A good example of such a mystery experience is the wonder and awe most everyone feels when just lying on their back in a field late at night and looking up at the clear night sky filled with millions of stars. The spirit always responds to this event, but that response is different for each of us. It is even different every time we undergo the experience. The experience of this spiritual transformation is the "mystery." The experience is vastly different than somebody telling us about it. And, of course, the experience for us is different than for anyone else. It also gives the one who discovers the mystery (that is, they experience the spiritual change within themselves) an enhanced connectedness to their own reality.

An explanation of what is expected to spiritually happen to the participants is a good way to describe the goal of the ritual. It prepares the ritual presenters for what is to come and gives them an idea of what to shoot for as a response from the people who attend the rite. After all, you would hardly expect an actor to deliver lines without telling him what sort of response you wanted from the audience. Similarly, those whose work it is to present the lines and set the mood of the ritual should be well aware of what their efforts are expected to produce.

The second step of any ritual is to establish the area. I knew when I began writing this where the rite would be taking place, so a portion of this step had already been done before the ritual was ever written. But the ritual's "establishing the area" is a way of making the chosen spot into a special place linked to this ritual. I have done this in the section labeled, **"PURIFICATION OF THE CIRCLE."** Starting at line 113, the **WARDER** is instructed to call out in a clear voice and tell everybody that the rite is beginning and that they are to be quiet. It is assumed that those who have gathered just outside of the stone circle will be watching and listening to what is going on inside the circle. If they do not observe what is happening, then the establishment of the circle is not nearly as powerful as it should be. The ritual presenters need to always keep a "weather eye" on the reactions of the people so they can tell if they are keeping the attention of everyone focused where they want it to be. This means that from the start, the presenters must be keenly aware of both the collective and individual energies of the people. This, of course, is true for every ritual.

At line 124, I have the **MAIDEN** take one of the traditional tools, the broom, and sweep in a counterclockwise spiral, from the center out, to signify the banishing aspect. Along with that, she is to recite a short rhyme that echoes her intent. This sort of words-and-action combination is used a lot so that everyone can be sure exactly what is supposed to be happening. I especially like to use this sort of thing when doing a public ritual because it leaves little room for confusion. I'm more comfortable when I know that even the most inexperienced will be able to understand what is going on. Rhyme is used in many of these sections because it makes things easier to memorize and it also has a way of "sticking" in the minds of people so that its meaning can have time to be "absorbed."

The next thing to be done in establishing the circle is once again done by the **MAIDEN** and her broom. This time (line 137), she sweeps in the opposite direction from what I had her do just a moment before. Then, she was banishing; now she is invoking, or "sweeping IN," which is another way of preparing the area. Notice on line 153 that I specify where she is to place the broom after she is done with it. I have made sure that it is placed in a spot where it will not be in the way of anything else that is to happen and will be ready to be used again at line 301. Attention to details like this is

84

one of the ways to cut down on confusion and reduce the chances of unexpected things happening.

Lines 159 through 185 are more establishment of the area. I have each **QUARTER CALLER** going to the central altar, picking up their symbol for the element they will be representing and walking around the circle once, using that element to establish the perimeter. This, by the way, is also a consecration of that area, at least in a limited fashion. It's not unheard of for an action or a symbol to serve more than one purpose simultaneously. In fact, by doing so, I have strengthened both purposes with one set of actions. This is not cutting corners; this is doubling the energy of the action.

When I wrote the statement that the **HP** makes while drawing the circle with the sword (191 - 200), I modified an often-used circle casting piece to focus on the goddess, Diana. In doing so, I've managed to direct people's minds back to the reasons they came to celebrate this rite. Never assume that everybody can keep their attention on something for very long. Most of us tend to drift after only a few minutes and if your rituals do not remind the participants on a regular basis, you will have them "yawning in the pews" before long. Once again, I've given very specific directions about where the tool the **HP** uses, the sword, is to be placed after he has used it to cast the circle. The significance of where the sword is laid and the direction it is pointing is to give the impression that the sword is guarding the gateway and actually completes the circle by pointing to where the **HP** started with his casting. Later, in lines 302 - 308, we see the sword being moved down and "sealing" the circle after everyone has been admitted. The **MAIDEN** also sweeps just in front of the gate before the sword is placed on the ground, once again symbolically making the impression of finalizing the establishment of the perimeter. The fact that the sword is sitting above the gate at line 204 makes a distinct portal of the gate even though the circle has been cast. Remember that the people are still standing outside of the stone circle on a path which is slightly above the level of the circle with a good view of everything going on.

Next comes a statement by the High Priestess (lines 209 -
211) commanding that the circle be warded. "Warding" is just
another way of saying she wants it to be made safe and that the
casting/sealing process is to be completed. This is most definitely a
consecration process (Step #3), for what the **QUARTER CALLERS** do
(lines 214 - 264) is to call upon the energies of the entire universe,
as represented by the four Elements. In their callings, the wording
of each Elemental call subtly reminds us of some part of the
purpose of the ritual. I worded these in a manner which was very
close to what had been used in many ceremonies in the greater
Seattle area. Since many of the people who would be coming to
this rite would be fairly new to the faith community, I figured I
would present the concept of calling the Elements in a way that
they would eventually find familiar in other circles they might
encounter later on.

Also, the wording of these calls is matched. That is, each of
the calls is six lines long, the first two of which are the same
wording except for changes in the direction and the Element being
called. The next four lines are the same format throughout each of
the four calls and were designed to explain to everyone exactly
what influences are being called into the circle. While this matching
is not always necessary to do, I thought it would help everyone if
these were easy to memorize and that they were clear in what was
being called upon. Unless it's really important to be esoteric or
mysterious, I prefer direct language, especially when the makeup of
the participants is relatively unknown.

The final part of the consecration process (Step #3) is the
anointing and blessing of the people. When the **MAIDEN** first put
up her broom, I had her pick up two vials of anointing oil and hand
one to the **WARDER**. At line 267, I have the **WARDER** go outside
the stone circle and up to the start of the line of people waiting to
be allowed into the circle. He is there to demonstrate by example
what the **HPS** will be telling the people to do before they enter the
circle. She tells everyone (beginning at line 276) to do a self-
anointing with water from the fountain. At the top of a rise
overlooking the circle, there stands a small fountain that is fed by

the pressure of the river. This fountain is a water pipe run up to the spot and allowed to constantly run through the small sculpted fountain and into a cup placed to catch the water. The cup can be removed and taken to drink or used on circle if need be. The water flows down the bank and partially around the outside of the stone circle, producing a small stream that must be crossed to enter the circle. The stream is only about a foot wide and easily crossed without getting footwear wet. The fountain, the cup, and the moat-like stream combine to make a happy, babbling sound that is added to the birds, the wind and the sunlight (or moonlight and stars) to make the stone circle a romantic and beautiful ritual spot. It has been traditional in past celebrations to use the waters from this fountain as a consecrative tool, so my use of them in this ritual is nothing more than staying with that tradition. The fountain makes a wonderful addition to the available energies of the ritual site and it would be foolish not to take advantage of it.

So the **HPS** tells them to anoint themselves, which is a form of consecration in and of itself. Then they are led down the four steps to cross the stream and enter into the stone circle. When they do, the **WARDER** and the **MAIDEN** do a second consecration with the oil on the forehead (lines 288 - 300) and the people form the circle around the inside of the stone circle. The final acts of the **MAIDEN** and **WARDER** are to sweep at the entry point of the circle and move the sword down on the ground. This is done after everyone has been welcomed into the circle and these actions signal the final "sealing" of the circle. Lines 316 through 322 sees the **HPS** declaring this so everyone understands that the circle is now fully cast and the area is set up for the rest of the rite. So, at line 327, she commands, *"LET THE RITE BEGIN."* To be technical, of course, the rite has already begun. But to have her say it is just a good way to get everyone together on what is to come rather than what has already been.

In fact, line 327 is the beginning of Step #4, the crystallization of the vision. By making that statement, the people get the idea that something is about to happen and they should pay attention. This helps to form them into a group rather than a collection of individuals and the **HP** gives them a short description of why the ritual is being held (332 - 338). The next portion (350 - 386) is named the **CALL TO MYSTERY**. Each person, upon entering the circle, was handed a small sheet of paper with this printed on it. If they were in a Protestant church, this section would probably be in a hymnal under the section labeled "Responsive Readings." The purpose is the same. It is to focus the people's thoughts onto the subject of why they are there and what is to be expected. This reading is both a form of crystallizing the vision as well as a preliminary to Step #5, raising the energy.

The **CALL TO MYSTERY** is formulated to echo the thoughts expressed in the Elemental calls used by the **QUARTER CALLERS** in lines 214 - 264. In this way, the people are also reinforcing the establishment of the circle (Step #2) as well as the consecration of it (Step #3). Thus, I have provided a method for them to become part of every step of the rite, even though they were outside the circle (as observers) for part of the opening portions. Also, the message within the **CALL TO MYSTERY** is a prelude to the mystery within the rite. In making a reference to the words that will be said later on, I've placed a false "memory" in the minds of everyone because they've already said the words in this part. When they run across these words in a slightly changed form again (in lines 447 - 460 in part "A" and 651 -671 in part "B"), they will seem familiar and the message will have a greater impact.

It might seem that I've spent very little time making sure that everyone has a consistent idea of what the ritual is all about. But you would be surprised to find how easy it is to get people working on the same "wavelength" if they work together. Having them do a responsive reading with words that are carefully selected is often more than enough to make individuals become a group with a common goal. Other methods of making people into a solid group are guided meditations, singing or chanting together, working on a common project (such as making something to be used later in the ritual), or any other activity that directs their attention toward the goal of the ritual. In the case in point, the responsive reading gets everyone saying things about the worship of Diana and what that means in terms that relate to the cosmos as defined by the four Elements plus the Element of Spirit (the center). Because they have said the words together, I've already given them a start at operating as a unified group with a personal investment in the ritual.

At this point, I've gotten the people prepared to witness and become part of the myth that will be presented to them. I am counting on the fact that I have involved the people enough with the preliminary steps that they will be willing, active, and focused participants in the rest of the ritual. The next step, of course, is to raise the energy. To do that, I present a play in which the **HPS**, who has received the energy raised during the **CALL TO MYSTERY** (oh yes, that part served more than one purpose also!), becomes the embodiment of Diana. This transformation begins with the **HP** calling on the spirit of Diana, enumerating her qualities that the ritual must utilize, and focusing everyone on the fact that the person who is acting as **HPS** will become that spirit (lines 403 - 416). Then the **HP** gets everyone to chant a very short and simple two line stanza over and over again (422 -425), designed to build the expectations and visualization on the part of each participant.

This part is very delicate. The **HPS** must be ultra-sensitive to just how effectively the chant is working. She must sense when the energy of the group has reached its peak and be able to absorb that energy at just the right moment. It is at that moment that she will rise up (431 - 442) and **be** the Goddess. If the **HPS** misses the timing on this or does not receive the energy properly and fails to present the Goddess, the rest of the ritual will not be nearly as effective as it should be. If everything works perfectly, the **MAIDEN** will place the crown on the head of Diana, **not** the **HPS**. Although I have choreographed the actions of the **MAIDEN**, **WARDER**, and the **HP** so they should act as if the Goddess has come into their midst, the actions will be totally natural only if the **HPS** has truly taken on the aspect of Diana. The people should also react this way. The Goddess has come into the body of the person who **was** the **HPS** and they will probably kneel also. If the Goddess has truly manifested through her priestess, this moment will be a stately, inspiring, and beautiful one.

Once the Goddess has manifested, it is entirely possible that the rest of the ritual, as I have written it, will go out the window. This is something of which I am very aware, for I've seen it happen. She who has become the Goddess may in fact be moved to produce a totally different mystery than the one so carefully planned by myself. This is **not** an "error." In the choosing of the persons to act as **HPS** and **HP**, it is essential that they both be able to react to one another in a natural and trusting manner. And it must be understood by both that such "diversions" as that which I have just mentioned do happen on occasion. If it does, the **HP** must respond appropriately to the Goddess and remember one of the responsibilities he has is to safeguard the psychological, emotional, and physical wellbeing of the **HPS** and the people on the circle. He must react to the Goddess in a way that enhances her actions, yet he must constantly be protective of the person and body of the **HPS**. Usually, the two jobs are one in the same. But occasionally the Goddess will overpower the priestess and the **HP** must be able to handle the situation with a weather eye on the welfare of both the **HPS** and the people who are subject to the influence of the Goddess.

What I am speaking about is something akin to what is mistakenly called "possession." The **HPS** has voluntarily sublimated her own personality to that of the Goddess' spirit. A miscalculation can tip the energy the wrong way. Although this **very rarely happens**, it still must be guarded against. A similar thing can also happen, though usually in a less potent fashion, to any who attend the rite. After all, the ritual is purposely designed to produce a psychological result in each participant. There will always be unknown factors that can upset even the most banal and impotent of rituals. If the people who present the ritual are not prepared to handle such circumstances, they should not attempt to perform the ritual.

But if things go as planned, the presentation of the mystery by the Goddess will trigger a change in the outlook of the participants. In ritual {A}, the mystery is presented starting at line 467. While the mystery is being presented, I've borrowed an old transformational chant from my own tradition that has a predictable result in nearly everybody. This chant starts out with everyone chanting one word: **MAYA**. Over that chant, the Goddess will be implanting some statements designed to cast new light on the mystery that is being presented (with the aid of the box). On about the second over-verse, the **HP** will change from chanting "**MAYA**" to "**I AM**." This is not at all obvious, for if you repeat "**MAYA**" over and over, you will be saying the same sounds as "**I AM**." So when the **HP** changes the words, he will not be changing the sounds and in a matter of moments, everyone else will be saying, "**I AM**" along with the **HP** but may not even realize it until later. This transformation of words without change in sounds will make it easier for those who are mentally and emotionally ready to experience a moment of dual understanding. It is much like seeing the classic silhouette of a chalice which is also the side view of two faces. You can see one or you can see the other. But it is rare and requires very special circumstances to see **both** at the same time. The **MAYA** chant is a way of facilitating such a moment. Combined with the other symbols of the ritual, this moment of hyper-awareness can radically change the entire outlook of a person. At such times, the symbolic experiences of the moment can make for a wondrous realignment of the entire psyche or a very frightening one. That is why a great deal of care should be taken to surround the person with symbols that will feel positive and safe.

At the conclusion of the passing of the box, the Goddess is allowed to leave the priestess (lines 550 - 561). Here is where I've pulled another subtle switch. In the offering of the pita bread (lines 572 - 579), I am relating forward to ritual {B} and implanting another false "memory." The response by the **HPS** (lines 587 - 590) echoes what goes on in ritual {B}. Those who have come to the Diana's Bow ritual at the ATC the month before will have encountered the {B} ritual, so they will be hearing the same line as they will hear in that ritual at lines 666 through 668. If they have not yet attended a {B} ritual, then hearing lines 587 - 590 will plant the words in their minds so that when the Goddess says them in {B} the next month, they will feel familiar.

In case you haven't figured it out yet, the box that Diana gives the High Priest to pass around has a mirror in the bottom of it. And the word, "MAYA," means magic. The transformation of "MAYA" into "I AM" while each person gazes into the box, presents a chance for that person to discover something new and sacred about their own being. This is the moment of the mystery. Of course, this will not be achieved with everyone, but by repeating the ritual every other month, the opportunity is available many times and the pressure to experience the mystery mounts with each successive presentation. If the person goes every month and partakes as the rituals alternate, the message of each becomes stronger with the participation in the alternate. Ritual {A} reinforces {B} which reinforces {A}, etc. So the more times a person attends, the stronger the overall effect becomes.

In the {B} ritual, dynamics similar to {A} are at work. However, the mystery that was presented in {A} is now turned inside out. In {A}, the participant was supposed to discover the mystery of self; in {B}, they are presented with the mystery of that self being part of a greater whole. Each ritual has the same beginning and end, thus making the two mysteries into a third which is their combination. Both versions of the rite connect to give an experience of who the person is, relative to their universe. This is one of the High Mysteries: "Who am I?" And, as any student of magic can tell you, the first commandment is to "know thyself."

The chant which begins at line 719 was inspired by a poem by the modern myth-maker, Jane Yolen. Her stories are wonderful tales that are really for grown up children. They inspire and beguile, but more than anything else, they take the reader into a new realm of wonder. This chant has been used many times by the people of my own coven and at several Pagan festivals. It can get quite lively and it is nearly impossible to stand still while doing it.

Once again, in lines 835 through 837, the words that were the key to the mystery of ritual {A} are said by the **HPS** in ritual {B}. The sections both in {A} and {B} that come immediately after the

Goddess has left the **HPS** are pure Step #7. They are to take the attention away from the events that were designed to focus, direct, and release the energy (Step #6), which is what the Goddess does by appearing at the ritual. It is difficult to separate the raising of the energy (Step #5) from the focusing, etc. of that energy. Nearly every action or word done from line 403 (in the unified beginning) through 543 in ritual {A} and 794 in ritual {B} has the dual duty of fulfilling both Step #5 and Step #6 simultaneously.

In each version, the **HPS** re-emerges and Step #7 (grounding the stray area) is begun. This starts at line 563 in {A} and line 809 in {B}. In most of the rituals I have created, I've taken a great deal more time to ground the stray energy. And I would have done a much more thorough job in this ritual except for one consideration: this ritual is for the purpose of generating interest in the church where it is held. I've purposely made the grounding somewhat incomplete. I **wanted** there to be left over energy after the rite is ended! It will be useful in helping to generate volunteerism and interest from the people who have attended the rite. In doing this, I am hoping that the people will leave the stone circle and want to find some place to put their excess energies. Since the church is right there for them to interact with, it is reasonable to hope they will decide to be more involved with church activities to satisfy their need for a place to expend their energies.

Both parts {A} and {B} reunite at line 853 with the **MAIDEN** giving the command to undo the wards. To enhance the notion that what was done to erect the circle is now being undone, I've used a time tested form of dismissing the wards in reverse order from how they were put up. So **NORTH** begins with a statement of thanks-and-good-bye to the Earth Element and the rest of the **QUARTER CALLERS** follow in reverse order of the opening. Their statements are designed to help the people remember what was called in for that Element at the beginning. And, of course, each of the **QUARTER CALLERS** holds up the symbol of their Element as before. The purposeful similarity between the calling in and the dismissal by the **CALLERS** is much more than whimsy. It is because the unmaking of the wards requires that the connections to the unconscious that were made in the beginning should be targeted by the actions and words of the dismissal. Otherwise, it is possible that the circle will not have been taken down in the minds of the people attending the ritual.

Every church that I have ever been in has some part of its services devoted to announcements and information about other events of interest to the people who attend. I did not want to put this part any place in the main body of the ritual where it would disrupt the flow of the ceremony. I had to find a spot where everyone could be distracted without it taking them away from the energies of the ritual. The natural place (line 912) was just before performing the very last action to take the circle down (line 937). Therefore, I put it after the Elements were dismissed and just before the **WARDER** uses the sword to dismiss the circle and people. Putting it there also helps everyone to regain their sense of the rite being ended and makes it more likely they will be paying attention. This is also where the **HP** makes a plea for money and help for the church.

While a great many public Pagan rituals are put on each and every month all over the country, very few ask for money in the same way a regular church would. Many of the larger events that celebrate the Greater and Lesser Sabbats are held in parks, campgrounds, or halls that charge a fee. They usually either break even or come close to it. The ATC, which commissioned me to create this ritual, also holds a couple of these each year. But the Pagan community is populated mostly with people who have become disenchanted with "regular" religions, which they often view as money grubbers, and it has become almost an unwritten rule that asking for money to support a ministry is a "cardinal sin" in the Pagan community. However, it's foolish to think that a few dedicated people should pick up the tab each month for such an operation. That is why I've written in that the **HP** needs to remind people that the church needs funds and volunteers.

Step #8, returning everything back to its previous condition, is only partially accomplished in the presence of everyone. For the general attendees, the final portion of this step is performed by the

WARDER in lines 643 through 646. Then the **WARDER** and the **MAIDEN** usher the people out of the circle and back down to the main building. But the final act of finishing the rite is done only by the ritual presenters, or "staff," as per lines 961 through 971. The seven line general dismissal that I've used here is one which my own High Priestess wrote many years ago. Since we began using it for our rituals, it has also spread to other circles and become almost "public domain" for many groups. Since the Arch Priest of the ATC questioned the word used in the last line (SHEM-HEM-PHOR-RASH), I would like to explain it. It is part of one of the Seals of Solomon (the Moon seal), a magical emblem from a book called ***The Lesser Key of Solomon***. The word is part of a Hebrew sentence which roughly translates as "find hidden treasure." It is used here by way of a reminder to everyone that we should actively look for the wonder, beauty, and true worth of the world around us, a fitting end to any work of magic.

The last paragraph of the written ritual is just a bit of in-house directions to clean up the stone circle altars and to mix with the people who attended the rite. Although the cleanup is certainly part of Step #8, the rest of the directions are more for the sake of anyone who may be presenting the ritual. I figured it couldn't hurt to put a few directions concerning the duties that the **HP** and the **HPS** take on as representatives of the church. In this and a few other significant aspects, this ritual departs from the usual Pagan rituals. This ritual is for a **church**, not a coven or circle. And the **HP** and **HPS** are acting as clergy, not just priest and priestess.

Well, there you have it, a complete breakdown and analysis of how the Eight Steps exist as an internal support structure for a particular ritual. As you have seen, not everything is done in steps of equal size, nor have all the steps been in exact order. But all the steps are there and if I could assign homework, I would ask that you take a ritual which you have observed and do your own analysis of it to see where each step is applied. In doing so, you may even be inspired to write a slightly different version of it yourself. Many rituals used in the Pagan community could use some improvement. However, until you are very experienced at ritual building, I would suggest that you get other people to critique any changes you think should be done so you don't embarrass yourself. It's easy enough to make changes that may look great on paper but end up being very wrong in reality. Experience, experience, experience, there is no substitute!

[19]

The Shallow End

Learning the various steps of ritual construction doesn't make you an instant master of the art. In fact, nothing you read will teach you as much as rolling up your sleeves and actually creating a ritual. But that's kind of like jumping into the pool at the deep end to see if you can swim. In all likelihood, you'll at least take a few mouthfuls of nasty tasting pool water that way. Much better if you step down in the shallow end and try things out where it's a lot safer, right?

Welcome to the shallow end. This chapter is designed to lead you through the process of creating a ritual. However, since I have no idea what purpose your rite will be for, it's going to be a little like going through a review of what all this book has covered, only in much shorter and less detailed form. Don't expect it to be of much help unless you have already read and understood what has been discussed before this chapter.

If you have gotten this far, you undoubtedly will have some idea about what your ritual should be about. You have this burning desire to jump right into the middle of this grand project and produce something that would put Cecil B. DeMille to shame. That's wonderful. Except you will find that constructing rituals that are truly beautiful and meaningful is a hard job. It will take about two hours of thinking, writing, rewriting, and *re*-rewriting to produce one minute of ritual. And when you think you are done, you'll be awakened at four o'clock in the morning with a "better idea" about it and you won't be able to go back to sleep until you write it into the "finished" script and, because you changed that part, some other part needs to be tweaked and then you read it over again and correct the misspelling here and the wording there and it all seems to be so complicated and difficult and you really want it to be just simple and beautiful and, and, and... OMG, it's 8 a.m. and you've got to get ready for work!

Begin by resolving that you won't panic. Your enthusiasm for making something beautiful and inspiring is a wonderful gift and it will serve you well. But remember also that you will be working on a project that can take a long time to produce something you can be proud to display. Whatever you pick as your first project, keep it small and simple. Some of the most used rituals are hardly longer than five seconds [the social ritual of a handshake, for instance], and some of the most beautiful can be only one word [Namaste]. Create your first ritual with heart and you will be proud of it the rest of your life. How big and grandiose won't matter an hour after it is done; how beautiful it is will.

Okay, here we go.

The first thing you need to do is pick a purpose for your first ritual. Before you settle on one, however, let me suggest that you don't pick something where you have a bunch of people attending. This puts unnecessary pressure on you and there's plenty of time later to try changing the universe for the benefit of all humankind. You could pick a holiday where only a few people attend, a dedication or ritual blessing of a tool or other magical item, a self-dedication [what some call a self-initiation], or any number of other purposes. As long as you feel it is *important*, it's probably worth doing and doing well.

All throughout this work, I've emphasized the importance of having a clear and complete idea of the purpose of your ritual. And you've learned how that purpose drives every other part of the ritual construction process. So, obviously, your first job is to figure out what the purpose will be. But that might not be what you've seen inside your thoughts or been somehow inspired to envision.

Regardless of the order in which the steps of ritual construction have been discussed in this book, the actual process of building a ritual doesn't follow such a smooth and logical path. Real art is somewhat messy that way. Although it's very true that you have to have a clear idea of the purpose/goal of your ritual, there will be times when you won't even be thinking about creating a rite and BANG! you'll get a vision or idea about *part* of a ritual or some really inspirational words. And perhaps you won't even have a clue

98

about what ritual your inspiration is for! This is what's meant by the phrase, "The Muse is upon you."

If you do get a flash of inspiration, *write it down*. Psychic events like that are messages from the unconscious mind and even if they don't make sense at the moment, they will at some point in the future and you will be very thankful that you took a moment to record them. If you get in the habit of writing down your thoughts before you begin to try and analyze them, you will be amazed at how brilliant your unconscious mind really is. Also, the more you try to keep from analyzing these ideas, the better you will become at actually recording them just the way they appeared to you from the unconscious.

Remember the way we become aware of sensations and thoughts is they originate in the unconscious first [where they acquire meaning] and then flow through a translating mechanism of some sort that changes them from raw symbols to rational, linear thoughts. Effective rituals reverse this flow and attempt to change our reality by changing the meaning of things. If we learn to "speak" the language of the unconscious, we will become better at the ritual construction process. By getting in the habit of writing down our flashes of inspiration as quickly as possible after they happen, we will be teaching ourselves unconscious-speak in the same way as what is termed 'immersion' for a spoken language. That's like being plunked down in the middle of a foreign country and left to your own devices to figure how to ask the locals, "Where's the bathroom?" So begin writing down your ideas no matter how strange they might seem.

A lot of my students, when given the task of writing their first ritual, choose a self-dedication rite. Although I've mentioned this as a possibility, I don't want you to choose it just because I mentioned it. Such a rite is often a very intense emotional experience and should not be taken on lightly. Simply *wanting* a self-dedication isn't a good reason for making that your very first ritual construction project.

But if you do choose that, let me re-emphasize that writing a ritual will put you through all of the changes the ritual will be designed to manifest... *and other changes that you might have edited out by the time the ritual is completed.* Always, always, *ALWAYS* draw a circle of psychic protection around yourself when constructing ritual.

Okay, enough of that; it's time to think about the purpose of your ritual. Without a clear understanding of that, we can't work effectively on the rest of the construction process. In your search for the meaning of the ritual, the real essence, use whatever means you have at hand to dig deep and understand what your statement means. The statement I've been using all along, "How it feels is what it means," can be easily turned around: What it means is how it feels. When you arrive at the real meaning of your ritual, you'll know how the ritual should feel. This will be a powerful moment for you. When trying to refine the purpose of your rite, you can use the inner two year old but I also suggest you talk honestly and openly with someone who knows you well. Someone that you can speak with candidly about such matters. Such comrades can help when trying to extract meaning from words.

Once you have found the true meaning of the ritual you are going to construct, you will have to figure out when and where it will take place. Will it be indoors or outdoors, night or day, open to anybody or a carefully selected group, during a particular time [year, month, day, hour], and a hundred other things about the space/time of the event. While you are thinking on these, you probably will also get some vision of how the "stage" will be set, how the people will be dressed, and whether you'll need music or special lighting, etc. Remember our birthday party? It isn't any more complicated than that but it certainly isn't any less important.

Of course, this all has to do with establishing the area for the ritual. It's housekeeping. When writing a ritual, don't forget to write down the details that will distinguish your ritual space from another's. Such details are an important part of your vision and they need to be conveyed to the presenters.

Here's another side note about this step: people will sometimes forget [or are just too lazy] to write down such details into their ritual. This could be for a variety of excuses but it doesn't matter. Even if you are the only person at the ritual, you should write down your ideas, *all* of them. There will likely come a time when you will want to review that ritual [maybe somebody else wants something like it or you want to copy part of it] and it's really hard to remember what your thoughts were five years after the fact. So... [wait for it]... WRITE IT DOWN!

In establishing the area for the attendees of your ritual, it's quite possible you will already be engaged in some activity that also serves to consecrate the area, the people, and all the "stuff" within that space. But I advise you to set aside a specific time and activity that will serve this function alone. Write it into the ritual so that everybody knows what is going on. Remember why this is a vital part of the ritual and honor it accordingly. Many traditional things, like sweeping, calling quarters and Elements, greeting people as they enter the circle, etc., can be interpreted as consecrating the articles, area, and people, but a specific consecration should be done after the area has been established and before you begin to build the energy.

All of what I term "housekeeping" steps can be done quickly as long as you've devised a way for them to be done efficiently. I once attended a ritual where it took nearly ten minutes to call the quarters... *each quarter!* It was all very impressive and the group that was putting it on did a nice job of it. But 40 minutes spent calling the watchtowers, the Elements, the guardian totem animals, and the Archangels was a little much for keeping the attention of better than 50 people [some of whom were rather new in the Pagan community]. I was yawning half way through South!

Keep your audience in mind and respect the fact that they have been kind enough to attend your ritual. Respect their time and energy as well as their presence.

The next step is to crystallize the vision. This is skipped over all too often because people think everybody has the same understanding of what the ritual is for because, hey, look, they showed up for it, right? Wrong. I've been married to my wife for over 35 years. We finish each other's sentences! And yet we constantly have to explain what we mean to each other in spite of all that. Understanding another person's *meaning* is something you have to work at. Be sure to do most of that work for the people who attend your rite or you won't get the results you're hoping for. And even if the ritual is for one person, even if it is for you alone, *do this step*. It also happens to be a great lead-in for raising and handling the energy part of your ritual.

And now we are at the point in the ritual where all the preparation has happened and it's time to roll up the sleeves and make magic. This is where the *art* in ritual makes a big difference. Knowing how to raise energy that can be useful to whomever is going to shape it and put it to use is not the same thing as knowing how to describe that within the script of the ritual. This is usually the place where the script begins to look more like a commentary. There are fewer lines to speak but more directions to follow. How you instruct the ritual presenters about raising, focusing, directing, and releasing the energy will be the key issue in the ritual's overall impact. There are many factors to consider:

- How many people will be involved in the energy production?
- Will they all be doing the same thing [recommended] or will it need some coordination [much more difficult]?
- If this involves ritual presenters going around individually to each attendee, have you split the duties up between the presenters so that everyone can be quickly served?
- Who is to be the energy director? [sort of like band conductor]
- Have you written instructions that might need to be given to the attendees? Did you script them into the written ritual?

The number of people you estimate will be present for the ritual has a great deal to do with how the energy production is accomplished. Having only a few people means that it would be easy to control the energy production and to keep it well focused and aimed. However, the amount of energy might be too low. The larger the group producing the energy, the more energy you'll get but the tradeoff is that it is more difficult to control.

And here's a tip about dealing with large groups of people. I'll use a simple example to illustrate. Let's say you were going to have everyone chant something while someone went around with mini-smores [yummy!] and prune juice [hey, I can pretend all I want, it doesn't have to make sense]. If you were to carry a tray with both the smores and juice on it around a circle of ten people, and then another circuit to collect the empty prune juice cups, how long do you think it would take? Maybe ten minutes? Okay, so how long would it take if you had 50 people? If this was a third grade math problem, the answer would be 50 minutes. But in real life, figure more like 100 minutes! Splitting up the job so the number served is much smaller per ritual presenter means that this act would not take forever and you wouldn't have everybody looking at their watch, waiting for the smores and prune juice guy to come around. Always consider how much time something takes. People get bored easily and it's difficult to get their attention back once it has been lost.

As mentioned earlier, the ritual presenters will need all the help they can get from your ritual script but they also need training and experience. You won't always be able to control who is going to be chosen to be the presenters, so do everything you can to communicate your vision and meaning as you write your ritual. And at no point is that so critical as in the energy portion.

Unless you *know* you will be the person managing the energy portion of your ritual, write in something about how to end the energy generation *and release that energy*. Don't fail to do this step. Making a sure and clean break with the energy isn't the best way to get things done right, it's the *only* way!

Again, grounding the stray energy should have something written about it in the body of the ritual script. And here's a pointer: up to this point, it's always been advisable and helpful to have smooth transitions from one step to the next. However, because you *want* a disruption in the energy flow at this point, I'd actually advise that write something that is a little abrupt and has little chance of being easily connected to the rest of the ritual that has preceded this section. You might also have one of the ritual presenters caution the attendees against discussing the ritual among themselves either on or off circle. Give them something to do that will distract them and make them focus on one or more of their physical senses.

The liturgy for our coven's tradition has several different ways to end rituals, but what matters most is that everyone knows the rite is done and the ritual space/time has ended. This is important for your ritual also. Write something that will make it clear the rite is over. Have the presenters say the words and do the actions you think are a good way to communicate the message that the people are released from that energy construct and free to go and do what they want.

Even though it probably has taken you only five to ten minutes to read this chapter, using it as a quick reminder of what you need to do to construct your first ritual will take anywhere from several hours [too quick; check your work] to several months [don't feel bad, it took me a year and a half to write a ritual once]. When you've "finished" your new ritual, it's time to have somebody else read it and make suggestions or give feedback. Don't be too thin skinned when getting feedback about your work. Everybody will have something different to say. Listen to them all and argue *with yourself* about the merits of each. At the very least, these will give you deeper insight into how the ritual will affect people.

Every ritual depends on the symbols used in it. Knowing how people respond to those symbols is absolutely necessary for you to construct good ritual. Since words are symbols and a good deal of nearly all religious rituals are made up of mostly words, having a good facility with words is also a requirement for strong, meaningful rituals. Every ritual you create will teach you more about how to construct better rituals. Use your experience and your best intentions to build truly meaningful spiritual rituals.

[20]
Not the End

If you are creating rituals for your fellow faith group members, you are doing the work of a priest or priestess. Be aware that you can only do this kind of work for a very limited amount of time before you *must* keep doing it. It will take over your life and set new priorities for you. In short, you will be unable to stop. You've heard of the willing sacrifice? Guess what: you are it. The spiritual life will be the altar upon which you will freely lay your heart. If you think that is overly dramatic, you will find it true even if you wish it otherwise.

Creating rituals is sacred work and if you are good at it, you will be called upon by many who need your art to help them in their own spiritual quest. Honor their trust with care and reverence.

The deeper you get into ritual creation, the more likely it is that you will begin to *produce* rituals. And even if you don't, you will quickly see the need for greater explanation to the ritual presenters about the aim of the ritual and how you believe its presentation should help attain that goal. I've already mentioned the idea of writing a commentary about the ritual after you have completed writing it. This commentary can be as long or as short as you consider necessary. The purpose of it is to assist the presenters with production of the rite in accord with your intent. I would also recommend creating a check list so that all the tools and props needed for the ritual are listed in one spot. When it comes time to set things up, those in charge will bless you, your family, and all of your cattle for writing up such a list.

Here are some other lessons I've learned over the years, in no particular order:

- Outdoor rituals are far more difficult to plan and execute than indoor ones.
- It is more difficult to do circle dances or other physical activities in the dark or low light than it is in the light.

- There's no harm in having a book handy with the ritual printed up. Even the Pope reads off most of his rituals.
- Technology can add much to any ritual if done correctly. But if it *can* go wrong, remember Murphy's Law.
- ***Always have a Plan B.***
- Candles are nice – but they can burn more than wax. And they can blow out, especially out of doors.
- Candles can give pretty light but aren't very good to read by. Always print up things that might need to be read in large print.
- Number your pages.
- ***Always have a Plan B.***
- When rehearsing a rite, try "playing" with delivery styles. You might find a better way of delivering the lines or stimulating the right emotion.
- The more complex the ritual, the easier it is to mess up.
- Did I mention you should always have a Plan B?

If you have studied the principles put forth in this book, you have probably discovered that a lot of what is termed "ritual" really isn't anything more than a play or even just a somewhat organized party. When you construct your first ritual from the bottom up, you find out just how much work goes into a major spiritual ritual, both in creating a script as well as presenting the rite for a group of people.

The knowledge in this book is not well understood by a large majority of the people involved in priestly or ministerial positions. Even those who teach religion are mostly unaware of the points put forth in these pages. The term "ritual" has so many different ways to be defined, it's no wonder there hasn't been any simple method of creating one until now. I have been criticized for over-simplifying what a ritual is and how it works within society and individual lives. But all of these criticisms are about *how the rituals are applied*. The system described here for creating rituals is completely neutral in both the application of the ritual as well as the cultural and spiritual source of it. These principles and methodologies aren't even just for religious rituals; they work for *all* rituals.

So you are now armed with powerful knowledge about one of humankind's most fundamental thought processes. There is nothing I can do or say from these pages to insure that you will use this knowledge for good instead of evil. However, I believe that any knowledge used for evil will end up biting the ass of the person using it that way. Everything is connected and every action has consequences.

I wish you well and hope this work has helped to make great beauty for yourself and others.

A.T.C.
DIANA'S BOW
RITUALS
"A" & "B"

These are the Mysteries to be discovered through ritual "A:"
- *If you do not find her within, surely you will never find her without.*
- *Strength of character comes from within.*
- *The God and the Goddess are within each of us; only in their union is the universe manifested.*
- *Worship of the God & Goddess is in service to the Life Force.*

These are the Mysteries to be discovered through Ritual "B:"
- *Only in the giving and receiving are the energies of the Universe multiplied.*
- *Service to the community is a Path of Enlightenment.*
- *The Dance of the God & Goddess is the Life Force of the Universe.*
- *Service to the Life Force of the Universe is worship of the God & Goddess within each of us.*

Each ritual is designed to enhance, complete, and give new meaning to the other as well as provide an opportunity by which one or more of

36 *the above named Mysteries can be*
37 *discovered by the participants.*
38
39 Purification of the Circle will take
40 place *before* the people are admitted.
41 The HPS or her deputy will pick those
42 amongst the people who have attended
43 before and who have expressed a desire
44 to be part of the ritual presenters by
45 performing the roles of Warder, Maiden,
46 and Quarter Callers. The Purification
47 takes place with the people observing
48 from outside the stone circle.
49
50 A full complement of ritual
51 presenters will be composed of: High
52 Priestess, High Priest, Maiden, Warder,
53 and 4 Quarter Callers. The purpose of
54 this arrangement is to establish a reward
55 and involvement goal for those who may
56 wish to go further than simply being part
57 of the "people" who come to the rituals.
58 The positions of Maiden and Warder will
59 be filled only by those who have gone
60 through all four Quarter Caller positions.
61 The ritual will be primarily presented by
62 the HPS and HP, but some parts may be
63 handed over to the Maiden and Warden
64 at the discretion of the HPS. It is even
65 possible, with the agreement of **both** the
66 HPS and the HP, for the parts of either
67 the HP or HPS to be performed by the
68 Maiden and Warden, but not both in the
69 same ritual.
70
71 For both rituals, many of the
72 parts will be the same. Where there are

73	differences, the parts will be labeled "**A**
74	and **B**." It is the responsibility of the HPS
75	to insure that all presentation parts are
76	filled *before* the 1st Call to Ritual is given.
77	That is, before the 1st Call is given, all
78	the personnel listed above *will be*
79	*prepared and in the stone circle*. The
80	Warder is instructed by the HPS to give
81	the 1st Call 15 minutes before the ritual
82	is to begin. The 1st Call will be heralded
83	from the bottom of the steps below the
84	Hot Tub. The Warder is to return to the
85	stone circle immediately after the 1st
86	Call is made. The 2nd Call to Ritual is
87	done by the Maiden from the balcony of
88	the Hot Tub building 10 minutes before
89	the ritual is to begin. She returns to the
90	stone circle immediately after giving the
91	2nd Call. The 3rd and Last Call to Ritual
92	is given 1 minute before the ritual is to
93	begin by the HP. This is given just
94	outside of the entrance to the stone
95	circle. He then returns to the stone
96	circle and the presenters place
97	themselves in position for the
98	Purification of the Temple:
99	The **HP** & **HPS** stand at altar, the
100	**HPS** is cloaked, completely covering
101	Diana Robe.
102	The **WARDER** stands by the Gate
103	(Northern side).
104	The **MAIDEN** takes up the Broom
105	and stands on the other side of the Gate
106	(Eastern side).
107	The **QUARTER CALLERS** stand
108	across the circle from the directions they
109	are to call.

110
111 **PURIFICATION OF THE CIRCLE**
112
113 **WARDER**: (CALLS IN A CLEAR,
114 LOUD VOICE)
115
116 **"THE TEMPLE IS ABOUT TO BE**
117 **ERECTED. LET ALL WHO ENTER IN BE**
118 **HERE OF THEIR OWN FREE WILL.**
119
120 **PRAY ALL BE SILENT WHILE THE**
121 **TEMPLE IS PURIFIED."**
122
123
124 **MAIDEN**: (TAKES UP BROOM
125 AND SWEEPS FROM CENTER OUT,
126 WIDDERSHINS)
127
128 **"ALL THINGS WHICH EVIL OR**
129 **MALIGNANT BE,**
130 **KNOW THIS PLACE IS NOT FOR**
131 **THEE.**
132 **BE THOU GONE! DEPART FROM**
133 **ME!**
134 **AND BY MY WILL, SO MOTE IT**
135 **BE!"**
136
137 (NOW SWEEPS FROM THE
138 OUTSIDE INWARD, DIOSIL)
139
140 **"RED SPIRITS AND BLACK,**
141 **WHITE SPIRITS AND GRAY,**
142 **COME YE, COME YE, COME**
143 **WHO MAY.**
144 **AROUND AND ABOUT,**
145 **THROUGH IN AND THROUGHOUT,**

146	**THE GOOD COME IN, AND THE**
147	**ILL _KEEP OUT!_**
148	
149	(**EVERYBODY** STOMPS TWICE ON
150	LAST TWO WORDS)
151	
152	
153	(RETURNS BROOM TO
154	EAST SIDE OF GATE, TAKES UP TWO
155	VIALS OF ANOINTING OIL AND HANDS
156	ONE TO WARDER)
157	
158	
159	**EAST**: (TAKES UP INCENSE
160	FROM ALTAR, LIGHTS CHARCOAL AND
161	PLACES INCENSE UPON IT, WALKS ONCE
162	AROUND CIRCLE, DIOSIL, AND STANDS IN
163	THE WEST TO CALL TOWARDS THE EAST)
164	
165	
166	**SOUTH**: (TAKES UP CANDLE
167	OR OIL LAMP FROM ALTAR, LIGHTS IT,
168	WALKS ONCE AROUND CIRCLE, DIOSIL,
169	AND STANDS IN THE NORTH TO CALL
170	TOWARDS THE SOUTH)
171	
172	
173	**WEST**: (TAKES UP
174	WATER FROM THE ALTAR, WALKS ONCE
175	AROUND CIRCLE, DIOSIL, SPRINKLING
176	WATER AS THEY WALK, AND STANDS IN
177	THE EAST TO CALL TOWARDS THE WEST)
178	
179	
180	**NORTH**: (TAKES UP SALT
181	FROM THE ALTAR, WALKS ONCE
182	AROUND CIRCLE, DIOSIL, SPREADING

183	SALT AROUND THE EDGE OF THE CIRCLE,
184	AND STANDS IN THE SOUTH TO CALL
185	TOWARDS THE NORTH)
186	
187	
188	**HP**: (TAKES SWORD AND
189	BEGINS AT THE EAST SIDE OF GATE)
190	
191	**"OH THOU CIRCLE, I CONJURE**
192	**THEE:**
193	**SACRED AREA OF MYSTERY,**
194	**A SHIELD AGAINST EVIL WILL**
195	**YOU BE,**
196	**AND CONTAIN WITHIN ALL**
197	**ENERGIES.**
198	**ALL THIS WE CLAIM BY THE**
199	**MAJESTY**
200	**OF** <u>**DIANA**</u>**! ... SO MOTE IT BE!**
201	
202	(ENDS AT THE NORTHERN
203	EDGE OF GATE AND PLACES SWORD
204	<u>ABOVE</u> THE GATE, POINTING TO EAST)
205	
206	**HPS**: (CLEARLY AND WITH
207	COMMAND TO HER VOICE)
208	
209	**"BY THE CONJURATION OF THE**
210	**ELEMENTS,**
211	**LET THIS CIRCLE BE WARDED!"**
212	
213	
214	**EAST**: (HOLDING INCENSE
215	UP ABOVE EYE LEVEL)
216	
217	**"GUARDIANS OF THE EAST,**
218	**ELEMENT OF AIR,**
219	**BREATH OF LIFE**

220	**AND WINDS OF INSPIRATION:**
221	**BLOW AWAY THE CLOUDS**
222	**FROM OUR MINDS**
223	**AND GIVE US TRUE VISION."**
224	
225	
226	**SOUTH**: (HOLDING FLAME UP
227	ABOVE EYE LEVEL)
228	
229	**"GUARDIANS OF THE SOUTH,**
230	**ELEMENT OF FIRE,**
231	**FLAME OF SELF**
232	**AND LIGHT OF**
233	**TRANSFORMATION:**
234	**ENERGIZE THE LIFE FORCE IN**
235	**OUR BODIES**
236	**AND GIVE US THE POWER TO**
237	**MAKE A CHANGE."**
238	
239	
240	**WEST**: (HOLDING THE
241	WATER UP ABOVE EYE LEVEL)
242	
243	**"GUARDIANS OF THE WEST,**
244	**ELEMENT OF WATER,**
245	**WAVES OF FEELING**
246	**AND OCEANS OF MEANING:**
247	**WASH AWAY OUR ANGER AND**
248	**FEARS**
249	**AND GIVE US PURITY OF LOVE**
250	**AND TRUST."**
251	
252	
253	**NORTH**: (HOLDING THE SALT
254	UP ABOVE EYE LEVEL)
255	
256	**"GUARDIANS OF THE NORTH,**

257   **ELEMENT OF EARTH,**
258   **FERTILE FIELDS OF SUSTENANCE**
259   **AND MOUNTAINS OF**
260   **TREASURE:**
261   **MANIFEST THE DREAMS AND**
262   **FEELINGS WE TOIL FOR**
263   **AND GIVE US VALUE IN OUR**
264   **LIVES.**
265
266
267   **WARDER**: (GOES TO THE START
268   OF THE LINE OF PEOPLE AND LEADS
269   THEM IN WHAT TO DO AS THE **HPS**
270   SPEAKS)
271
272
273   **HPS**:   (STANDING IN
274   CENTER, FACING PEOPLE)
275
276   **"THE ELEMENTS ARE IN**
277   **BALANCE, WHICH BRINGS SPIRIT TO THE**
278   **CIRCLE.**
279
280   **"CHILDREN OF THE GODDESS**
281   **AND THE GOD, BLESS AND PURIFY**
282   **YOURSELVES. ANOINT YOUR HEAD,**
283   **HEART, AND LOINS WITH THE WATERS**
284   **OF LIFE AND COME ONTO THIS CIRCLE**
285   **OF WORSHIP IN PEACE."**
286
287
288   **WARDER & MAIDEN**:   (HE
289   LEADS THE PEOPLE TO THE GATE AND
290   STANDS AT NORTHERN SIDE OF GATE,
291   SHE AT THE EASTERN SIDE, AND THEY
292   WELCOME EACH PERSON IN WITH A
293   PENTACLE ON THE FOREHEAD, DRAWN

294	IN SCENTED OIL, AND THE WORDS,
295	**"Thou art God(dess),"** HE TO THE
296	FEMALES, SHE TO THE MALES. THE
297	PEOPLE ARE LED AROUND THE INSIDE,
298	DIOSIL, UNTIL THEY ARE AT THE BACK OF
299	THE WARDER... THUS THE CIRCLE IS
300	FORMED. WHEN ALL HAVE ENTERED,
301	THE **MAIDEN** WILL SWEEP IN FRONT OF
302	THE GATE AND THE **WARDER** WILL TAKE
303	THE SWORD AND LAY IT ON THE
304	GROUND **(to protect the sword, a tarp**
305	**or some other suitable wrap may be**
306	**placed upon the ground under and over**
307	**the sword)** IN FRONT OF THE GATE,
308	POINTED TOWARDS THE EAST. HE WILL
309	STAND IN FRONT OF THE SWORD AND
310	WARD THE GATE FOR THE REST OF THE
311	RITUAL.)
312	
313	
314	<u>HPS</u>: (TO ALL THE PEOPLE)
315	
316	**"THE TEMPLE IS WARDED,**
317	**BLESSED, AND SEALED. IF ANYONE**
318	**FEELS THEY MUST LEAVE BEFORE THIS**
319	**RITE IS CONCLUDED, SILENTLY GO TO**
320	**THE GATE FROM WHENCE YOU**
321	**ENTERED AND HAVE THE WARDER GIVE**
322	**YOU EXIT. DO _NOT_ BREAK THE CIRCLE.**
323	
324	(PAUSE 5 HEARTBEATS AND
325	_SEE_ THE PEOPLE)
326	
327	**_"LET THE RITE BEGIN!"_**
328	
329	
330	<u>HP</u>: (TO EVERYONE)

331
332   "IT IS THE TIME OF DIANA'S
333   BOW. HER CRESCENT IS VISIBLE IN THE
334   SUNSET SKY AND IT IS THE BOW OF THE
335   HUNTRESS. IT IS THE TIME OF
336   BEGINNINGS. LET THIS RITUAL BE A
337   WORSHIP OF HER AND OF *YOUR*
338   BEGINNINGS.
339
340   "HELP ME CALL HER TO THIS
341   RITE. LOOK TO YOUR *ORDER OF*
342   *SERVICE* SHEETS AND SAY THE WORDS
343   OF THE READING ENTITLED *CALL TO*
344   *MYSTERY*."
345
346
347   - CALL TO MYSTERY -
348
349
350   **HP:**   WE SEEK DIANA,
351   HUNTRESS OF THE NIGHT
352   EAST
353   **ALL:**   GIVE US TRUE
354   VISION THIS MAGICAL NIGHT
355
356
357
358   **HP:**   OUR HANDS AND
359   HEARTS EMPOWER THIS CALL
360   SOUTH
361   **ALL:**   WE FIND HER
362   WITHIN, OR NOT AT ALL
363
364
365
366   **HP:**   HEART JOINED TO
367   HEART AND LIP TO LIP

```
368          WEST
369          ALL:          FIVE ARE THE
370   POINTS OF FELLOWSHIP
371
372
373
374          HP:          SOW THE SEEDS
375   DEEP IN FERTILE GROUND
376          NORTH
377          ALL:     LET THE WHEEL
378   CARRY US ROUND AND ROUND
379
380
381
382          HP:     HARMONY AND
383   BALANCE ARE THE WAY TO POWER
384          CENTER
385          ALL:     WE SEE THIS TRUTH IN
386   EVERY TREE AND FLOWER
387
388
389
390               - THE CALLING -
391
392
393          HP:          (GOES TO HPS, KISSES
394   HER RIGHT HAND, AND WALKS HER TO
395   THE CENTER.  HE HAS HER KNEEL WITH
396   RIGHT KNEE ON THE GROUND, HEAD
397   DOWN.  THE crescent crown IS
398   BROUGHT FROM THE ALTAR BY THE
399   MAIDEN AND HELD OVER THE BOWED
400   HEAD OF THE HPS FROM IN BACK OF
401   HER AS THE CALLING IS MADE.)
402
403          "HAIL DIANA, HUNTRESS OF THE
404   NIGHT,
```

405	GODDESS OF THE MOON, BLESS
406	THIS RITE.
407	
408	"OH DIANA, YOUR PRIESTESS
409	WILLINGLY GIVES HER BODY AND
410	HEART SO THAT YOU MAY WALK IN THE
411	CIRCLE OF STARS WE HAVE FORMED TO
412	WORSHIP YOU, GODDESS OF GROVES
413	AND WELLS. COME, OH COME,
414	MAJESTIC DIANA. COME UNTO THIS
415	RITE AND BEGIN AGAIN THE MYSTERY
416	OF THE NIGHT!"
417	
418	(START EVERYONE CHANTING)
419	
420	
421	**ALL**: (CHANT)
422	*"HAIL DIANA, HUNTRESS OF THE*
423	*NIGHT,*
424	*GODDESS OF THE MOON, BLESS*
425	*THIS RITE."*
426	
427	{A}
428	
429	**HPS**: (WHEN THE PEOPLE HAVE
430	BUILT A SUFFICIENT ENERGY LEVEL THE
431	**HPS** WILL RISE UP, DROPPING HER
432	CLOAK, AND THE GODDESS WILL BE
433	UPON HER. THE **MAIDEN** WILL PLACE
434	THE CROWN UPON HER HEAD, TAKE
435	AWAY THE CLOAK, AND FADE BACK TO
436	STAND BESIDE THE WARDER. THE **HP**
437	WILL KNEEL BEFORE THE GODDESS,
438	HEAD BOWED. THEN THE **WARDER** AND
439	THE **MAIDEN** WILL ALSO KNEEL, BUT
440	STAY LOOKING AT THE CIRCLE AND THE

441 GODDESS. WHEN THE GODDESS SAYS
442 TO RISE UP, ALL THREE WILL DO SO.)
443
444   "RISE UP MY CHILDREN; LOOK
445 AT ME STRAIGHT AND TRUE.
446
447   "I AM SHE WHO NEEDS NO
448 OTHER FOR SUPPORT. I AM WITHIN
449 EACH AND ALL OF YOU, BOTH HIGH
450 AND LOW. I AM SHE WHO BEGINS NEW
451 PLANS, GIVES NEW HOPE, AND
452 SUSTAINS THE SELF AGAINST
453 IMPOSSIBLE ODDS. *LOOK AT ME!* YOU
454 HAVE CALLED ME INTO THIS FORM
455 TONIGHT, BUT I HAVE BEEN WITH YOU
456 ALWAYS! *I* DO NOT NEED THIS MORTAL
457 FORM FOR *YOU* TO RECEIVE MY
458 BLESSING, *FOR IF YOU DO NOT FIND ME*
459 *WITHIN, SURELY YOU WILL NEVER FIND*
460 *ME WITHOUT*."
461
462   (SHE UNCOVERS A BOX, WHICH
463 SHE HAS HAD IN A SLING-PURSE OVER
464 HER SHOULDER, AND HANDS IT TO THE
465 **HP**.)
466
467   "THIS IS MY GIFT TO YOU ALL,
468 MY CHILDREN. WITHIN THIS BOX IS MY
469 TRUE FACE AND FORM. GAZE INSIDE
470 AND REMEMBER SO YOU MAY
471 RECOGNIZE ME WHEN IN NEED OF MY
472 BLESSINGS. AND IF YOU ARE SO IN
473 NEED, JUST SAY THE NAME OF THIS
474 BOX, WHICH IS... *MAYA*."
475
476

121

477 **HP**: (BEGINS CHANT AND
478 GETS ALL TO JOIN IN. WHEN EVERYBODY
479 HAS JOINED THE CHANT, HE WILL BEGIN
480 WITH THE **MAIDEN** AND SHOW THE
481 CONTENTS OF THE BOX TO EVERYONE
482 INDIVIDUALLY, OPENING AND CLOSING
483 THE BOX FOR EACH. WHEN HE IS PART
484 WAY AROUND THE CIRCLE, THE
485 GODDESS WILL START HER CHANT. HE
486 SHOWS THE CONTENTS OF THE BOX
487 LAST TO THE **WARDER**.)
488
489 *"MAYA... MAYA... MAYA...*
490 *MAYA... ..."*
491
492 (ABOUT THE MIDDLE OF
493 THE SECOND VERSE, THE **HP** WILL
494 CHANGE WHAT HE IS CHANTING TO: *"I*
495 *AM... I AM... I AM... I AM... ....*)
496
497
498 **HPS**: (WHILE OTHERS ARE
499 CHANTING)
500
501 - MAYA -
502 (my' ah)
503
504
505 I am the Wolf, but do not fear
506 me...
507
508 I am the Hunter, and you do not
509 hear me.
510
511
512 I am the Blind One, you cannot
513 save me...

514
515   I am the Wild One, you will not
516   brave me.
517
518
519   I am the Path and you cannot
520   find me...
521
522   I am your Fear but you will not
523   bind me.
524
525
526   I am your Pain and you will not
527   free me...
528
529   I am your Shadow, you refuse to
530   see me.
531
532
533   I am the Dark Pit and your soul
534   will feed me...
535
536   I am the Gods but if you won't
537   claim me,
538
539   Seal up your heart and never
540   more blame me.
541
542   I AM... I AM... I AM... I AM... I
543   AM... I AM.......
544
545
546   **HPS**:   (AFTER THE BOX IS
547   GIVEN BACK TO THE GODDESS BY THE
548   **HP**.)
549

550   **"NOW IT IS TIME FOR ME TO**
551   **RESUME MY HUNT. LOOK TO THE SKY**
552   **EACH NIGHT AND WATCH AS I PULL MY**
553   **BOW STRING. AS IT IS PULLED BACK,**
554   **MORE OF MY POWER IS AVAILABLE TO**
555   **EACH OF YOU. USE IT WELL.**
556
557   **"MY BLESSINGS TO YOU ALL.**
558   **LET THE MYSTERY OF THIS CIRCLE LIVE**
559   **ON IN THE DAYS AND NIGHTS TO COME.**
560
561   **"FAREWELL."**
562
563   (SHE KNEELS BACK DOWN,
564   AGAIN WITH THE RIGHT KNEE ON THE
565   GROUND, AND BOWS HER HEAD. THE
566   **MAIDEN** COMES AND TAKES THE
567   CROWN AND REPLACES THE CLOAK. THE
568   CROWN IS THEN PLACED UPON THE
569   ALTAR.)
570
571
572   **HP**:   (TAKES A PIECE OF
573   PITA BREAD FROM ALTAR. CROUCHES
574   DOWN AND TAKES BOTH HANDS OF THE
575   **HPS** AND ASSISTS HER BACK UPRIGHT.)
576
577   **"RISE UP MY PRIESTESS AND**
578   **TAKE THIS SACRAMENT OF SHE WHOM**
579   **YOU HAVE SERVED SO WELL."**
580
581
582   **HPS:**   (TAKES A BITE OF
583   PITA BREAD FROM THE HP AND THEN
584   TEARS A PIECE OFF FOR HIM AND FEEDS
585   IT TO HIM WITH THESE WORDS :)
586

587   **"THANK YOU, MY PRIEST. AND I**
588   **WOULD SHARE WITH YOU. FOR ONLY**
589   **IN THE GIVING AND RECEIVING ARE THE**
590   **FORCES OF THE UNIVERSE MULTIPLIED.**
591
592   **"BLESSED BE."**
593
594   (TURNS TO THE <u>MAIDEN</u>
595   AND SAYS :)
596
597   **"THE RITE IS DONE. DISMISS**
598   **THE CIRCLE!"**
599
600   **(CONTINUED UNDER "{BOTH A**
601   **& B}")**
602
603
604   **{B}**
605
606
607   <u>**HPS**</u>:   (WHEN THE PEOPLE
608   HAVE BUILT A SUFFICIENT ENERGY LEVEL
609   THE **HPS** WILL RISE UP, DROPPING HER
610   CLOAK, AND THE GODDESS WILL BE
611   UPON HER. THE **MAIDEN** WILL PLACE
612   THE CROWN UPON HER HEAD, TAKE
613   AWAY THE CLOAK AND FADE BACK TO
614   STAND BESIDE THE WARDER. THE **HP**
615   WILL KNEEL BEFORE THE GODDESS,
616   HEAD BOWED. THEN THE **WARDER** AND
617   THE **MAIDEN** WILL ALSO KNEEL, BUT
618   STAY LOOKING AT THE CIRCLE AND THE
619   GODDESS. WHEN THE GODDESS SAYS
620   TO RISE UP, ALL THREE WILL DO SO.)
621
622   **"RISE UP MY CHILDREN; LOOK**
623   **AT ME STRAIGHT AND TRUE.**

624

625   **WHY HAVE YOU CALLED ME**

626   **FROM MY HUNT? WHAT IS IT YOU**

627   **NEED THAT YOU CAN'T PROVIDE FOR**

628   **YOURSELF? SPEAK TRULY, PRIEST, OF**

629   **THE NEEDS OF YOUR PEOPLE."**

630

631

632   **HP**: (LOOKS AROUND THE

633   CIRCLE AS IF ASSESSING THE PEOPLES'

634   NEEDS.)

635

636   **"WE HAVE GATHERED HERE TO**

637   **RENEW OURSELVES THROUGH**

638   **WORSHIP OF YOU, OH DIANA. WE**

639   **BESEECH YOU TO GIVE US ENERGY TO**

640   **GO ON IN OUR LIVES. YOUR CRESCENT**

641   **IN THE EVENING IS OUR SIGN OF HOPE.**

642   **TEACH US YOUR SECRETS OF HOW TO**

643   **SUSTAIN OURSELVES WITHOUT**

644   **DEPENDENCE. WE ASK ONLY THIS."**

645

646

647   **HPS**: (LOOKS AROUND AS

648   IF TO SEE IF THE PRIEST HAS SPOKEN

649   TRUE)

650

651   **"SO, YOU THINK THAT I CAN**

652   **GIVE YOU ENERGY? YOU SEE ME ALONE**

653   **IN MY HUNT, BUT YOU DO NOT SEE**

654   **CLEARLY.**

655

656   **"WHAT IS MY HUNT WITHOUT**

657   **THE QUARRY? WHAT ARE MY ARROWS**

658   **WITHOUT THEIR TARGET? WHAT IS**

659   **YOUR WORSHIP WITHOUT ME? *WHAT***

660   ***AM I WITHOUT YOU?!?***

661
662   "YOU CAN'T GIVE WORSHIP TO
663 ME WITHOUT MY RECEIVING IT. I CAN'T
664 *BE* WORSHIPPED WITHOUT GIVING IT
665 BACK TO YOU. OF ALL THE MYSTERIES,
666 THIS IS THE GREATEST: *ONLY IN THE*
667 *GIVING AND RECEIVING ARE THE*
668 *FORCES OF NATURE MULTIPLIED.* YOU
669 CAN'T GIVE THAT WHICH YOU HAVE
670 NOT RECEIVED, NOR CAN YOU RECEIVE
671 THAT WHICH YOU CAN'T GIVE.
672
673   (SHE REACHES OUT HER LEFT
674 HAND TO THE **HP**, WHO RESPONDS BY
675 REACHING OUT HIS RIGHT HAND AND
676 GRASPING HERS.)
677
678   "IF IT IS ENERGY YOU WANT, IT
679 IS ENERGY YOU MUST GIVE. I CAN'T
680 HOLD YOUR HAND IF YOU WILL NOT
681 HOLD MINE.
682
683   "NOW HOLD OUT YOUR HAND
684 TO ANOTHER... AND THEY TO THE NEXT
685 AND THE NEXT AND THE NEXT."
686
687   (THE **HP** GOES TO THE PERSON
688 JUST EAST OF THE **MAIDEN** AND TAKES
689 THEIR RIGHT HAND WITH HIS LEFT.
690 THEN, AS SOON AS EVERYONE HAS
691 JOINED HANDS, THE GODDESS SPEAKS
692 AGAIN.)
693
694
695   **HPS**:
696

697	**"AND NOW WE WILL DANCE**
698	**THE DANCE OF LIFE. IF ANY CAN'T**
699	**DANCE WITH US, JUST SIT AND PUT OUT**
700	**YOUR HAND AND I WILL TOUCH YOURS**
701	**AS WE GO BY."**
702	
703	(A SPIRAL DANCE WILL LEAD THE
704	PEOPLE IN A PATTERN THAT MAKES THE
705	LEAD END UP ON THE NORTHERN SIDE
706	OF THE GATE AND EVERYONE HAS
707	REVERSED THEIR DIRECTION ALONG THE
708	CIRCLE. IN OTHER WORDS, THE PERSON
709	THAT *WAS* TO THEIR RIGHT IS NOW ON
710	THEIR LEFT. THE **WARDER** AND **MAIDEN**
711	WILL REMAIN IN PLACE. THEY MAY BEAT
712	A DRUM IF THEY CAN KEEP THE RHYTHM
713	SET BY THE GODDESS. THE **QUARTER**
714	**CALLERS** WILL ALSO STAY IN PLACE. *ALL*
715	WILL CHANT.)
716	
717	(THE **HPS** BEGINS THE CHANT:)
718	
719	***"TOUCH MAGIC, PASS IT ON***
720	(STOMP, STOMP!)*... TOUCH MAGIC,*
721	***PASS IT ON*** (STOMP, STOMP!) ***TOUCH***
722	***MAGIC, PASS IT ON*** (STOMP, STOMP!)*...*
723	***TOUCH MAGIC, PASS IT ON*** (STOMP,
724	STOMP!)*... ."*
725	
726	
727	**HPS:** (LETS GO OF **HP**'s
728	HAND AND MOVES TO CENTER ONCE
729	AGAIN. **HP** AND **MAIDEN** COME TO
730	CENTER TO ATTEND HER *AFTER* SHE HAS
731	STARTED TO RUMMAGE IN HER PURSE-
732	SLING. SHE WILL PULL OUT PITA BREADS

733	AND HOLD THEM OUT TO THE **HP** AND
734	**MAIDEN**. SHE THEN ADDRESSES THEM :)
735	
736	**"TAKE THIS BREAD."**
737	
738	(THEY BOTH TAKE SEVERAL
739	PIECES. THEN SHE ADDRESSES THE
740	PEOPLE.)
741	
742	**"AS A SIGN THAT YOU ARE**
743	**WILLING TO BOTH GIVE AND RECEIVE,**
744	**TAKE A PIECE OF THIS BREAD AND FEED**
745	**IT TO THE PERSON NEXT TO YOU.**
746	**WHILE YOU DO THIS, LOOK DEEPLY**
747	**INTO THEIR EYES AND SEE ME THERE.**
748	**WHILE ANOTHER IS GIVING THIS TO**
749	**YOU, LOOK BACK INTO THEIR EYES AND**
750	**RECOGNIZE THE HOLINESS OF *THEIR***
751	**SOUL. IN WORSHIP OF THAT DIVINE**
752	**SPARK WITHIN ANOTHER, YOU GIVE**
753	**TRUE WORSHIP TO ME... *AND I TO***
754	***YOU*!**
755	
756	**"BE BOTH GIVER AND RECEIVER**
757	**AND YOU WILL BE ABLE TO LIVE YOUR**
758	**LIVES IN HARMONY WITH THE**
759	**UNIVERSE."**
760	
761	
762	**HP** AND **MAIDEN**
763	(DISTRIBUTE THE BREAD. THE **HP**
764	WILL BEGIN WITH THE **WEST QUARTER**
765	**CALLER** (who stands in the east) AND
766	THE **MAIDEN** WILL BEGIN WITH THE
767	**EAST QUARTER CALLER** (who stands in
768	the west). BOTH WILL TEAR OFF A
769	SMALL PIECE OF THE BREAD AND FEED IT

770   TO THEIR RESPECTIVE CALLERS, THEN
771   HAND THE BREAD TO THE PERSON THEY
772   HAVE JUST FED. THAT PERSON WILL
773   TURN TO THE PERSON ON THEIR LEFT
774   AND REPEAT THIS ACTION, AND SO ON.
775   WHEN ALL HAVE BOTH GIVEN AND
776   RECEIVED, THE **HP** AND **MAIDEN** ARE
777   FED BY THE PERSON WHO STANDS TO
778   THE RIGHT OF THEIR RESPECTIVE
779   CALLERS. THEY THEN GO TO THE
780   CENTER AND FEED EACH OTHER, HER
781   FEEDING HIM FIRST. THEN THEY TURN
782   BACK TO THE GODDESS AND OFFER THE
783   REMAINING PIECES OF BREAD TO HER.)
784
785
786   **HPS**:   (SHAKES HER HEAD
787   AND HOLDS UP HER HANDS IN REFUSAL.)
788
789   **"NO. YOU HAVE ALREADY**
790   **GIVEN WORSHIP TO ME. GIVE WHAT**
791   **REMAINS TO THE LAND AND THE**
792   **ANIMALS THAT LIVE IN MY GROVES.**
793   **GIVE BACK TO THE EARTH, FOR YOU**
794   **HAVE RECEIVED MUCH FROM HER.**
795
796   **"NOW IT IS TIME FOR ME TO**
797   **RESUME MY HUNT. LOOK TO THE SKY**
798   **EACH NIGHT AND WATCH AS I PULL MY**
799   **BOW STRING. AS IT IS PULLED BACK,**
800   **MORE OF MY POWER IS AVAILABLE TO**
801   **EACH OF YOU. USE IT WELL.**
802
803   **"MY BLESSINGS TO YOU ALL.**
804   **LET THE MYSTERY OF THIS CIRCLE LIVE**
805   **ON IN THE DAYS AND NIGHTS TO COME.**
806

807	**"FAREWELL."**
808	
809	(SHE KNEELS BACK DOWN,
810	AGAIN WITH THE RIGHT KNEE ON THE
811	GROUND, AND BOWS HER HEAD. THE
812	**MAIDEN** COMES AND TAKES THE
813	CROWN AND REPLACES THE CLOAK. THE
814	CROWN IS THEN PLACED UPON THE
815	ALTAR.)
816	
817	
818	**HP**: (CROUCHES DOWN
819	AND TAKES BOTH HANDS OF THE **HPS**
820	AND ASSISTS HER BACK UPRIGHT.)
821	
822	**"RISE UP MY PRIESTESS. THE**
823	**GODDESS WHOM YOU HAVE SERVED SO**
824	**WELL HAS LEFT YOU. LET ME SHARE**
825	**HER SACRAMENT WITH YOU."**
826	
827	
828	**HPS:** (TAKES A BITE AND
829	THEN TEARS A PIECE OFF FOR HIM AND
830	FEEDS IT TO HIM WITH THESE WORDS:)
831	
832	**"THANK YOU, MY PRIEST. AND I**
833	**WOULD SHARE WITH YOU. BUT WE ARE**
834	**WRONG TO THINK THAT SHE IS GONE.**
835	**SHE IS HERE WITH US ALL. FOR IF YOU**
836	**CAN'T FIND HER WITHIN, SURELY YOU**
837	**WILL NEVER FIND HER WITHOUT.**
838	
839	**"BLESSED BE."**
840	
841	(TURNS TO **MAIDEN** AND SAYS:)
842	

843	"THE RITE IS DONE, DISMISS THE
844	CIRCLE."
845	
846	
847	{BOTH A & B}
848	
849	
850	**MAIDEN**: (POINTS TO THE
851	**NORTH QUARTER CALLER** AND SAYS :)
852	
853	"UNDO THE WARDS! BEGIN AT
854	THE ENDING AND END AT THE
855	BEGINNING!"
856	
857	
858	**NORTH**: (HOLDS UP SALT AS
859	BEFORE.)
860	
861	"GUARDIANS OF THE NORTH,
862	ELEMENT OF EARTH:
863	WE THANK YOU FOR THE
864	WEALTH YOU HAVE PROVIDED.
865	GO BACK TO YOUR REALMS
866	WITH OUR BLESSINGS IN PEACE.
867	HAIL AND FAREWELL!"
868	
869	
870	**WEST**: (HOLDS UP
871	WATER AS BEFORE.)
872	
873	"GUARDIANS OF THE WEST,
874	ELEMENT OF WATER,
875	WE THANK YOU FOR THE
876	MEANING YOU HAVE GIVEN TO US.
877	GO BACK TO YOUR REALMS
878	WITH OUR BLESSINGS IN PEACE.
879	HAIL AND FAREWELL!"

880
881
882   **SOUTH**:   (HOLDS UP FLAME AS
883   BEFORE)
884
885   **"GUARDIANS OF THE SOUTH,**
886   **ELEMENT OF FIRE,**
887   **WE THANK YOU FOR THE FIRES**
888   **YOU HAVE KINDLED WITHIN US.**
889   **GO BACK TO YOUR REALMS**
890   **WITH OUR BLESSINGS IN PEACE.**
891   **HAIL AND FAREWELL!"**
892
893
894   **EAST**:   (HOLDS UP INCENSE
895   AS BEFORE)
896
897   **"GUARDIANS OF THE EAST,**
898   **ELEMENT OF AIR,**
899   **WE THANK YOU FOR YOUR**
900   **INSPIRATION AND VISION.**
901   **GO BACK TO YOUR REALMS**
902   **WITH OUR BLESSINGS IN PEACE.**
903   **HAIL AND FAREWELL!"**
904
905
906   **HP**:   (TAKES UP NOTES.)
907
908   **"THERE ARE SOME**
909   **ANNOUNCEMENTS AND REMINDERS**
910   **YOU SHOULD BE MADE AWARE OF:"**
911
912   (THIS IS THE TIME FOR
913   ANNOUNCEMENTS, PLUGS FOR FUTURE
914   **ATC** EVENTS, A LESSON, ETC. THIS IS
915   ALSO THE TIME TO REMIND THE PEOPLE
916   THAT THE **ATC** DOESN'T RUN ON AIR,

917 BUT NEEDS FINANCIAL SUPPORT AND
918 THE WILLING HANDS OF MANY.
919 ENVELOPES WILL BE PASSED OUT AND
920 EVERYONE IS ENCOURAGED TO GIVE
921 INTO THE PLATE HELD BY THE **MAIDEN**
922 AT THE FOOT OF THE STAIRS OR IN THE
923 COLLECTION BOX IN THE **RETREAT**
924 **HOUSE** BEFORE THEY LEAVE. ALSO, IF
925 ANYONE IS INTERESTED IN BECOMING
926 MORE INVOLVED IN THE RITUALS
927 AND/OR ACTIVITIES OF THE **ATC**, PLEASE
928 TALK TO THE **HPS** OR THE **HP** DURING
929 THE SOCIAL HOUR.)
930
931
932   **WARDER**: (TAKES UP SWORD
933 AND WALKS TO THE CENTER. HOLDS
934 SWORD POINTING STRAIGHT UP, ARM
935 FULLY EXTENDED, AND SAYS :)
936
937   **"THE CIRCLE IS OPEN,**
938   **BUT NEVER BROKEN.**
939   **MERRY MEET AND MERRY**
940 **PART,**
941   **AND MERRY MEET AGAIN!"**
942
943
944   (THE **WARDER** HANDS THE
945 SWORD TO THE **HP** AND WALKS TO THE
946 GATE TO USHER OUT THE PEOPLE. THE
947 **MAIDEN** NOW LEAVES TO STAND AT
948 BASE OF STAIRS WITH THE COLLECTION
949 PLATE. WHEN SHE HAS DISAPPEARED
950 FROM SIGHT, THE FIRST PERSON NORTH
951 OF THE GATE LEAVES FIRST, FOLLOWED
952 BY THE REST OF THE LINE OF PEOPLE.)
953

954
955   **HPS:**   (WHEN EVERYONE
956   HAS DEPARTED, THE RITUAL STAFF WILL
957   GATHER IN THE CENTER OF THE CIRCLE,
958   RAISE THEIR HANDS INTO THE AIR AND
959   SAY WITH THE **HPS** :)
960
961   **"OH SPRITS WHOM THIS CIRCLE**
962   **HAS DRAWN,**
963   **WE THANK THEE AND ASK THAT**
964   **YOU NOW BE GONE.**
965   **BACK TO YOUR REALMS WITH**
966   **OUR BLESSINGS IN PEACE,**
967   **AS WE DO WILL, SO MOTE IT BE.**
968   **WITH POINTS DRAWN DOWN,**
969   **WE MAKE THE SLASH,**
970   **EACH TO THEIR OWN:**
971   **SHEM-HEM-PHOR-RASH!"**
972
973   (ALL RITUAL GEAR, PROPS, ETC.
974   ARE GATHERED UP BY EVERYONE AND
975   TAKEN BACK TO THE HOUSE. IT IS THE
976   DUTY OF THE HPS AND THE HP TO MIX
977   WITH THE PEOPLE IN A "SOCIAL HOUR."
978   THEY WILL REMAIN IN THEIR ROBES
979   UNTIL AFTER THE SOCIALIZING IS DONE.
980   THE MAIDEN AND THE WARDER MAY DO
981   LIKEWISE. THE QUARTER CALLERS ARE
982   INSTRUCTED TO GET BACK INTO THEIR
983   STREET CLOTHES A.S.A.P. AFTER THE
984   RITUAL IS ENDED. EXACTLY 45 MINUTES
985   AFTER THE RITUAL HAS ENDED, THE HP
986   WILL ANNOUNCE THAT PEOPLE SHOULD
987   CLEAN UP, REMOVE ANY ARTICLES AND
988   POT LUCK DISHES AND FOOD THEY MAY
989   HAVE BROUGHT WITH THEM AND
990   PREPARE TO LEAVE FOR THE EVENING.

991   EXACTLY ONE HOUR AFTER THE RITUAL
992   HAS ENDED, THE <u>HP</u> WILL ANNOUNCE
993   THAT THE CHURCH IS CLOSED AND
994   EVERYONE SHOULD LEAVE, THANK YOU
995   AND GOOD NIGHT.)

ABOUT THE AUTHOR

Blacksun wrote another book about ritual construction back in the 1990's titled, *The Spell of Making* which is no longer in print. This work is a more streamlined version of and it is hoped that publishing it in both hard copy as well as e-book will make the information more available to all wishing to create new rituals.

A Wiccan priest, teacher, author, and speaker for over 40 years, Blacksun lives near Seattle, Washington with his wife and two dogs. He has also written four fiction books, *Dead Man's Hand, The Hannut Scrolls, Dark Thoughts*, and *The Once and Future Witch*.

Also look for his book on the fifth Element (Spirit) titled *Be ALL!* as well as *My Little Book of Pagan Magic* and a collection of talks and lectures on a variety of Pagan related topics, *Chats From a Comfy Chair*.

Made in the USA
Monee, IL
05 February 2023

27149829R10083